PREACHING CHRIST IN CORINTH

Exegetical-Homiletical Sermon Outlines
on First Corinthians

BY

KLAAS JACOB STRATEMEIER Th.D

Pastor German Presbyterian Church, Grundy Center, Iowa

ZONDERVAN PUBLISHING HOUSE
GRAND RAPIDS   MICHIGAN

Copyright, mcmxxxvi, By
ZONDERVAN PUBLISHING HOUSE

Grand Rapids, Michigan
813-15 Franklin St., S. E.

Printed in U .S. A.

THE PERSON

Christ! I am Christ's, and let the name suffice you;
Aye, for me too He greatly hath sufficed,
Lo, with no winning words I would entice you,
Paul has no honour, and no friend but Christ.

THE PREACHER

Would I describe a preacher, such as Paul
Were he on earth, would hear, approve, and own,
Paul should himself direct me. I would trace
His master strokes, and draw from his design.
I would express him simple, grave, sincere;
In doctrine uncorrupt; in language plain;
And plain in manner; decent, solemn, chaste,
And natural in gesture; much impress'd
Himself, as conscious of his awful charge,
And anxious mainly that the flock he feeds
May feel it too; affectionate in look,
And tender in address, as well becomes
A messenger of grace to guilty men.

He, stablishes the strong, restores the weak,
Reclaims the wanderer, binds the broken heart,
And, arm'd himself in panoply complete
Of heavenly temper, furnishes with arms,
Bright as his own, and trains, by every rule
Of holy discipline, to glorious war,
The sacramental host of God's elect.

Cowper, The Task.

PREFACE

A first reading of the treatise of Karl Barth on First Corinthians aroused in me the desire to preach a series of sermons on this Epistle and thus to impart to my congregation the challenging message of this Pauline letter. The reading of the English translation of Barth's work confirmed me in this purpose and left me no peace until the plan had been carried out. I shall never regret the labour and effort bestowed upon this series of sermons. Their preaching was marked by a fine response. The working out of the message immensely widened the outlook of preacher and congregation and served to establish the hearers in the fundamental Christian truths.

The attempt to preach continuously through entire books of the Bible has the sanction of both ancient and modern usage. We are in line with a great tradition when we concentrate preaching upon larger portions of Scripture. The "homilies" of the Church Fathers followed this method. The great Reformers loved to preach continuously on several chapters or even entire books of the Bible. Amongst the moderns Karl Barth stands out as a proponent of this form of preaching. The latest messages issued by him under the general title "Theological Existence Today" indicate his love for this vehicle of Biblical interpretation. Rightly handled it proves to be a very effective way in which to set forth the whole counsel of God.

Through the influence of the "Crisis" theology new emphasis has been placed upon expository preaching.

Karl Barth in Germany and E. G. Homrighausen in America insist that we must give a larger place to exegesis in our pulpit work. Our topical preaching has left the preacher barren and the man in the pew empty. The exegetical-homiletical method of preaching is to be much preferred because it proves itself a better channel through which the irresistible flow of Divine revelation surges to flood mind and heart of the hearer with an exhilarating experience of grace and glory.

To serve this end these outlines have been planned and cast into their present form. They will lend themselves to adaptation should a practical demand call for briefer treatment. Their one aim is to stimulate interest in the great message of the Apostle and to provide an outlet by which this magnificent array of Christian truth shall find its way into the Church of to-day.

Klaas Jacob Stratemeier.

Grundy Center, Iowa.

ACKNOWLEDGMENTS

Recognition is due, first of all, to "The Expositor's Greek Testament." In the preparation of these outlines this work has been constantly before us. To the student of the New Testament it is simply indispensable. In his commendable little volume "The Pastor as Student and Literary Worker" (Concordia Publishing House, 1925) Dr. Th. Graebner of St. Louis makes repeated reference to this commentary as providing a real basis for pulpit work and on page fifty-three quotes Dr. Dau as saying: "No English Lutheran who is engaged in the studies of the Scriptures in the vernacular can afford to ignore the condensed results of the studies of reputed scholars throughout the world which are offered him in this book."

The trend of First Corinthians is best seen by reading Karl Barth's volume on the Epistle published under the title: "The Resurrection from the Dead." (English translation published by the Fleming H. Revell Company, 1933. One gets much closer to the thought of the author however by reading the German original. It appeared in 1924. While termed by Barth—humbly enough—as a class room lecture on 1 Cor. 15, it offers an almost complete interpretation of the entire epistle. Seldom does one find an exegetical volume so thrilling and captivating. We have had occasion several times to correct the translation by reference to the German original. Barth offers a fresh approach to the understanding of the Epistle which will be welcomed by open minds and devout thinkers. A master exegete is at work here and, while baffling at times, his comments are always provocative of earnest thought looking for practical application in the life of the

Church. There are many surprising turns, details are seen in a new light, but the real burden of the message is never lost sight of. While shocked by the stark reality of conditions described, one rejoices in the indomitable hope ever pushed into the foreground by this treatise of Barth. "Christ is risen indeed," and that makes all the difference in the world.

The explanatory and practical "Notes" by Albert Barnes are still serviceable. The amount of practical material embedded in these notes is simply astounding. Calm and conservative in nature the verse by verse comments of Barnes merit attention. They are clear and consistent. Saturated with a deep devotional fervor these notes have great practical value and help much to bring the message of the Epistle close to the life of the Church.

A very recent work on First Corinthians came to our desk early enough to have a part in the preparation of these outlines. The aged scholar Dr. A. Schlatter has given us his exegetical work on First Corinthians (including also the second Epistle) under the title: *Paulus, der Bote Jesus.* Schlatter devotes 461 pages to the First Epistle. The Greek text is always in his mind, but the commentary abounds in practical considerations arising out of a real understanding of the conditions prevalent in the Corinthian church and the situations faced by the Church at the present time.

Other works have been consulted as the outlines will reveal. To get the setting of a certain portion of the message we have frequently called in a recognized authority speaking to the topic under consideration. Due credit has been given these authors whenever cited.

CONTENTS

		I Cor.	Page
I	Called in the Fellowship	1:1-9	11
II	Contentions or Christ, which?	1:10-17	14
III	The Word of the Cross	1:18-21	17
IV	The Man and his Message	2:1-16	20
V	Co-workers in the Service of God	3:1-9	24
VI	Where are you Building?	3:10-23	28
VII	The Minister's Place before Man and God	4:1-21	32
VIII	Moral Earnestness	5:1-13	35
IX	The Christian in Relation to Law and the Natural Life	6:1-20	40
X	Should One Marry?	7:1-40	46
XI	Knowledge in Relation to Christian Conduct	8:1-13	51
XII	Self-Denial Practically Demonstrated	9:1-27	55
XIII	Idolatry in the Light of History and Contemporary Church Customs	10:1-33	60
XIV	Decorum at Church and the Communion Table	11:1-34	66
XV	The *E Pluribus Unum* of Spiritual Endowments	12:1-31	72
XVI	The Greatest Dynamic — Love	13:1-13	77
XVII	Edifying Speech	14:1-40	82
XVIII	The Resurrection of Christ in the the Experience of the First Believers	15:1-11	87
XIX	The Resurrection of Christ as the Essential Element of the Christian Faith	15:12-34	94
XX	The Resurrection as a Triumphal Arch	15:35-59	103
XXI	The Resurrection Faith in Daily Life	16:1-24	110

I.

CALLED INTO THE FELLOWSHIP

I Cor. 1:1-9.

Introduction:—

Let us note the beginnings of the church in Corinth as reported in Acts 18:1-21. Note the apostle's association with Aquila and Priscilla, the nature of his testimony: "Jesus is the Christ," the opposition, Paul's decision: "I go unto the Gentiles," the winning of Crispus "ruler of the synagogue," Paul strengthened by a vision of "much people," his months of ministry.

At Ephesus he has received the report concerning the condition of the church. There are party divisions, moral laxity needs correction, doctrinal matters need clearing up. All these problems are met by this epistle, sent from Ephesus 54 A.D.

This first section, 1:1-9, speaks concerning:

I. *The Fact of Fellowship.*

1. Is witnessed to by the writer: "Paul," with his Damascus road experience; the "Apostle," insisting on his authority as one commissioned by the Lord, knowing himself placed by "the will of God." "Sosthenes," receives mentioning, not as fellow composer of the letter, but as a fellow witness to the same Gospel.

2. Is central in the life of the church, which being "the church of God" is not an ordinary assembly, but a gathering of the called out citizens of the heavenly kingdom. The church "in Corinth," think of it! Here commerce thrives, currents of thought surge through the populace, moral lapses are made attractive by union with idolatrous worship. Here you have Boston, Chicago and Hollywood combined. Yet this is a church called into the fellowship —, it stands related to the founder, its members are "sanctified in Christ Jesus," they are "called to be saints." Nor do they stand alone, but in living union "with all that call upon the name of our Lord Jesus Christ in every place." The circle is widely drawn, church union is a present fact, where Christ is central. I believe in the communion of saints.
3. Is enhanced by the Apostolic benediction. The ordinary "greeting" receives a higher connotation. How much we need that "grace," redemptive, sustaining. And the gift of "peace" will be worth more than all understanding. Think of Goethe's sigh: "Thou, which of the heavens art, peace, peace, come into my soul," and the reply sent him: "Peace I leave with you, my peace I give unto you: not as the world giveth, give I unto you." John 14:27.

II. *The Effect of Fellowship.*
1. If the fellowship has been effective it is not to boast in it as being man's work, it is rather an

occasion of prayer. So Paul begins: "I thank my God concerning you."
2. This fellowship has enriched the believers in all utterance and all knowledge. The church thrives not on cleverness, but on spirituality.
3. This fellowship has confirmed the testimony of Christ. Closeness to Christ results in convictions and the faith of our fathers lives in spite of dungeon, fire and sword.
4. This fellowship has been effective in a practical way. "Ye come behind in no gift." We are saved to serve.
5. The enduring quality of the fellowship will reveal itself in the day of judgment. Religious vitality itself is no guarantee of Christian perseverance. Lift the eyes above the subjective gifts to the Giver of all these good things.

Conclusion:—

How comforting to know that God is faithful! What cause for giving thanks! Human excellence is unstable. We are confirmed not by our fidelity to God, but through God's fidelity to us. "He loves us better than we do ourselves." *F. W. Robertson.*

II.

CONTENTIONS OR CHRIST, WHICH?

I Cor. 1:10-17.

Introduction:—

Paul loses no time in coming to the things that trouble the Corinthian church. Questions of doctrine or discipline had better be settled as quickly as possible. Beware of compromise. Let there be no weakening of doctrinal standards. An emasculated Gospel will help nobody. Always magnify Christ and His redemption. In the presence of Calvary and the empty tomb trivialities have no place. Contentions are best met by a reaffirmation of essential truths. Note how Paul meets the situation:

I. *The Appeal to Unity.*
  1. Paul makes his appeal as one who has the welfare of the church at heart. "I beseech you." As apostle he might command, as a fellow-Christian he pleads.
  2. His appeal is in "the name of our Lord Jesus Christ," not on personal grounds, not for his, but for Christ's sake he would see matters improved.
  3. The idea of unity is stressed. Note the several expressions employed: "all," "speak the same thing," be perfected together "in the same mind," and "in the same judgment." How closely that approaches unto the original idea of unity in the

primitive church. Acts 2:42f; 4:32f.
4. A schism is a rent in the church, an injury to the fabric. Paul's appeal calls upon them to join thought and action for a united stand, which will enable the church to act as one body and to pursue Christ's work with undivided strength. *E.G.T.*

II. *The Basis of Facts.*
1. Paul has the facts in hand. "It had been signified unto me." The verb "signified" (Greek — edelothe) implies definite information, the disclosure of facts. *E.G.T.* Make sure of the facts, before you attack any problem in the church.
2. The facts have been furnished "by them of the household of Chloe," "an Ephesian woman known to the Corinthians whose people had been at Corinth and returned to Ephesus." *E.G.T.*
3. Paul's charges do not rest upon surmises, or upon reports of talebearers, nor upon stories peddled by just anybody. He can cite definite sources of information.

III. *The Position of the Parties.*
1. Paul can name the divisionists. They have labelled themselves.
2. The parties seek to justify their actions by appeal to the leaders:
   a) I am of Paul. It would be natural to push the name of the founder into the foreground. But Paul points away from self to Christ.
   b) I am of Apollos — far more brilliant than Paul. A. would appeal to the Greeks. A. himself was humble enough.

  c) I am of Cephas. Some would cling to the great preacher of Pentecost.
  d) I am of Christ. This party made capital of the highest name. What Pharisaic assumption!

IV. *The Impossibility of a Divided Church.*
 1. Can Christ be divided?
 2. Was Paul crucified for you?
 3. Baptism too, points not to the minister, but to Christ.

V. *The True Basis of Union.*
 1. Give open way and full sway to the Gospel.
 2. The cross is the central fact of word and life.

Conclusion:—
 1. Party spirit is essential selfishness.
 2. Correct the spirit of contention by a new emphasis on the cross of Christ.

III.

THE WORD OF THE CROSS

I Cor. 1:18-21

Introduction:—
1. We are prepared for this point in the argument. We have seen
    a) Fact and effect of fellowship in Christ.
    b) The factors that disturb this fellowship.
    c) Here we come to the basis of this fellowship.
2. This word is timely, because
    a) of the indifference to the fact of the cross.
    b) of the ignorance of the power of the cross.
    c) of the opposition to the preaching of the cross.
3. This message is central:
    a) in the teaching of the New Testament. (J. Denny, The Death of Christ.)
    b) in evangelical preaching. (Herrick Johnson, The Ideal Ministry, Chap. VI.)
    c) in Christian experience and life.

I. *The Cross creates a Crisis.* vv. 18-19
   1. Its rejection is the greatest peace of foolishness and will lead to doom. v. 18a.
   2. Its acceptance will save and issue in power. v. 18b. "Saved men are the Gospel's apology." *E. G. T.*
   3. Sacred history sounds warnings of like judgments coming to those that refuse God's wisdom. Is. 29:14. v. 19.

4. The cross is the clearest exponent of the two classes described also in the first Psalm and in Matthew 7:24-27.
5. Sense this crisis as you read Luther and Calvin and especially the theology of Crisis. Listen to Karl Barth: "The Kingdom of God has its beginning on the other side of the Cross, beyond all that is called 'religion' and 'life,' beyond conservatism and radicalism, physics and metaphysics." Rom. 5:6.

II. *The Cross exposes false Wisdom.* vv. 20-21
1. The word of the cross surpasses human philosophy. v. 20.
2. Not by reasoning, but by faith are we saved. v. 21.
3. God uses the "foolishness of preaching" as a means to lead men the way of the cross. The "term signifies not the act of proclamation, but the message proclaimed." *E.G.T.* v. 21.

III. *The Cross is more engaging than Signs and Speculations.* vv. 22-25
1. It meets the Jewish craving for signs and the Greek cry for wisdom by providing something far surpassing both. v. 22.
2. The message calls for consistency in its proclamation. v. 23.
3. The saved know the power of the cross. v. 24.
4. The superiority of this message lies in the fact that it is "of God." vv. 24, 25.

IV. *The Cross leaves no room for Self-glorification. Let us glory in the Lord.* vv. 21-31

1. Behold your calling, brethren. v. 26.
2. The fact of God's choice eliminates the glory of self. vv. 27-29.
3. We are existent only "of God" and "in Christ Jesus."
4. In Christ our redemption is quite complete. v. 30.
5. Not the Christian, but Christ is the proper object of glory. v. 31.

Conclusion:—

When I survey the wondrous Cross,
  On which the Prince of Glory died,
My richest gain I count but loss,
  And pour contempt on all my pride.

IV.

THE MAN AND HIS MESSAGE

I Cor. 2:1-16

Introduction:—

The man and the message are inseparable and both must be related to the central theme "Jesus Christ and him crucified."

Our times too call for a great message. "When the chariot of humanity gets stuck, as it has done now, nothing will lift it out except great preaching that goes straight to the mind and heart." *David Lloyd George.*

The man and the message are one in the dependence upon the Holy Spirit, as the later section of our passage shows. It is well that it be so. "The cross can never be fully seen until the light of the Holy Ghost is thrown upon it. The ambassador's instructions are clear. He must be guided by the Holy Ghost." So Chapman writes and continues: "The other day I heard of a clergyman who was not a great preacher, as the world calls preaching, but whose church was packed to the doors, and to whom God gave many souls, and a friend of his told the secret when he said, 'We could always hear him saying softly as he mounted the pulpit, "I believe in the Holy Ghost, I believe in the Holy Ghost."'" (The Ministers' Handicap, p. 73.)

Let us then consider Paul's Message; and observe:

I. *The Manner in which it was presented.* 1-5.
   1. Paul spoke not as a rhetorician. "Not with excellencey of speech." "We are not in the pulpit to give literary treats or any other kind of treat." "It is our business to transmit to men the Word of God." (Richard Roberts, The Preacher as a Man of Letters. pp. 207, 198.)
   2. Paul spoke with the determination to make the message plain. "I determined." In contrast of the fondness of Greek orators for flowery extravagances of speech.
   3. Paul spoke moved by a singular object: "to preach Christ crucified."
   4. Paul spoke conscious of his own limitations, as witnessing "in weakness, and in fear, and in much trembling."
   5. Paul spoke not in "persuasive words," but "in demonstration of the Spirit and power." He spoke conscious of the "testimonium Spiritus sancta." John 15:26. I John 5:7. Persuade he did as can be seen from II Cor. 5:11 and Acts 26:28, but not to triumph in speech however, but in order to lead men to Christ.
   6. Paul spoke as desiring that responsive faith should be grounded not in the wisdom of men, but "in the power of God."
II. *The Mystery which it was to disclose.* 6-9.
   1. This mystery is not comprehended by ordinary wisdom.
   2. This mystery relates itself to the life of "the Lord of Glory." Grammatically this is the geni-

tive of characteristic quality and means: "The Lord to whom glory belongs as His native right." (See Warfield, The Lord of Glory, p. 224.) Christ is the Glory of God, the Shekinah: God manifest to men. (p. 265.)
3. This mystery was never sensed by the rulers: Caiphas, the Sanhedrin, Pilate etc.
4. This mystery stands revealed to the lovers of God. They know themselves blessed by the things "God hath prepared," such as "pardon of sin, atonement, justification by faith, peace and joy." And if on earth the gospel confers such blessings on its friends, how much higher and purer shall be the joys which it shall bestow in heaven." (Barnes Notes ad loc.)
5. This mystery transcends ordinary understanding and observation. "Tye saw not, and ear heard not." R.V. "All the world had been strangers to this until God made a revelation to His people by His Spirit." *Barnes.*

III. *The Method by which it was delivered and to be understood.* 10-16.
1. It is a supernatural disclosure (apekalypsen) *E.G.T.* Knowledge of these things is through the revealing Spirit. v. 10.
2. He discloses for He first discovers. v. 10. "This is the Intelligence everywhere active, everywhere penetrating. The Spirit is the organ of mutual understanding between man and God. Rom. 8:16-26. These deeplaid counsels centre in Christ, and are shared by Him (Matt. 11:2; John 5:20; 17:10-

25); so that it is *one* thing to have the Spirit who "sounds the deeps of God," and "to have the mind of Christ." v. 16. *E.G.T.*
3. Human consciousness detects human behavior. God's things must be communicated to us by the Holy Spirit or we shall never know them.
4. Consider what favor *we* have received when the Spirit opened our eyes to know the things freely given us of God. v. 12.
5. The mode of utterance agrees with the character of the revealing Spirit. v. 13.
6. The unspiritual are deaf to the music of redeeming grace. v. 14.
7. Enlightened by the Holy Spirit we shall rightly relate the things revealed. The unspiritual man cannot understand or appreciate the hopes and fears and joys of the man led by the Spirit of God.
8. We have no understanding except as the mind of Christ becomes known to us through the Holy Spirit. v. 16. "Christ lives and thinks in the spiritual (II Cor. 13:3ff; John 15:1-8); the *unio mystica* is the heart of Paul's experiences." *E.G.T.*

V.

CO-WORKERS IN THE SERVICE OF GOD

I Cor. 3:1-9

Introduction: —

"The Christian life is the most comprehensive life known; it is as deep as the heart; it is as wide as the world; and it is as high as heaven."

"Every human being is travelling every day in one direction or the other — either upward toward the highest place that man can reach, or downward the lowest level to which man can fall; Christ gives us a vision of our possibilities and the strength to realize them." (William Jennings Bryan, "In His Image." pp. 137, 139.)

What is expected of those that would unite their interests and actions in doing the work which God would have them do? Our text provides the answer:

I. *They need to be spiritually minded.* vv.1-3.
  1. We are so often handicapped by the opposition of the carnal to the spiritual. The conditions of the Corinthian church demonstrate definitely the incapacity of the unspiritual for spiritual things. We still have to battle with these sinful tendencies.
  2. The carnal mind resists spiritual instruction and calls for milk instead of bread. Many are ready to hear a clever discourse, but fail to appreciate

the richer spiritual provisions in Christ. Is not spiritual immaturity a most prevalent condition amongst us?
3. Such carnal mindedness is a great breeder of discontent and leads to division and strife.
4. That attitude is reflected also in conduct. One cannot long think along a certain line, without also walking accordingly. v. 3.

II. *They need to look beyond the human factor unto the fact of God.* vv.4-6.
1. There is a place for human endeavor. Planting and watering the vineyard are no small jobs. (Joseph Parker: "Preaching is self-murder; it is shedding of blood.")
2. Ability to perform a work within the church is the equipment of grace. "Each as the Lord gave to him." v. 3.
3. Neither the planter nor the waterer are sufficient in themselves, God must give the increase. v. 7. Never lose sight of the dominating idea "of God." The utter dependence on God is always before the Apostle's mind. Without Him we can do nothing. Equipped by Him we can fill the place assigned to us.
3. As is the labor so will be the reward. v. 8.

III. *They need to remind themselves that they are God's possessions.*
1. They are God's fellow-workers. Give this phrase its right accent. Read it not as if God needed help. By the help of God we may work in fellowship together for Him.

main design and scope of this whole passage is to show that God is all — that the apostles are nothing; to respresent the apostles not as joint-workers with God, but as working by themselves, and God as alone giving efficiency to all that was done." "The apostles were joint-labourers with each other in God's service." *Barnes.* "The work of the diakonos would be improperly conceived as a Mit-arbeitin relation to God; moreover the metaphors which follow exclude the thought of such a fellow-working." *E.G.T.*

2. They are God's husbandry, God's farm. "My Father is the husbandman." John 15:1.

"It is a perfect metaphor — the soil of our personality made fruitful by the influences of heaven rained upon them. Commerce with the sky is the secret of productive life."

"The words bring to mind also the wide varieties of "farms" God has to work upon. Some are as fertile and luxurant as an opulent river bottom. Some are like the slanting field of the New England mountain-side, full of bolders, with a thick crust almost impervious to rain and sunshine, which grudgingly yields only a scrubby, scraggly growth. On some of God's farms the soil is exhausted; life is never replenished. On others the weeds have strangled any useful growth. You are God's farm. What kind of farm does He have?" (Halford E. Luccock, Preaching Values in New Translations of the New Testament," pp. 256-257.)

3. They are God's building. Comp. Heb. 3:4; 11:10.

"Of the two images, "farm" implies the organic growth of the church, "building" the mutual adaptation of its parts." *E.G.T.*

Conclusion:—

"Realizing God's all-comprehending rights in His Church, the too human Corinthians (3f) will come to think justly of His ministers." *E.G.T.*

VI.

WHERE ARE YOU BUILDING?

I Cor. 3:10-23

Introduction:—

a) This passage takes up the thread of v. 9 ("God's building"), and elaborates upon it.

b) How is the Church of God being built? Enthusiasm has a ready response. Will this enthusiasm take the direction of real spiritual building?

c) This building is everyone's responsibility, not in the sense that everybody's business is nobody's business, but with the emphasis that the individual is held accountable to God.

d) We are to work as spiritual architects, building upon the plans provided by God.

I. *The Church as founded on Christ.* vv. 10-15.

1. The apostle is sure that he is building upon this foundation. By the grace of God he did this wisely. "He was like the old cathedral builders." "The work of the Apostolic founders is done, once for ever; so long as the church lasts, men will build on what they laid down." *E.G.T.*

2. "There is but one foundation, and it is Jesus Christ." *E.G.T.* Frequent reference is made to this fact. Is. 28:16; Matt. 21:42; Acts 4:11; Eph. 2:20; II Tim. 1:19; I Peter 2:6. "No true church

can be reared which does not embrace and hold the true doctrines respecting Him." *Barnes*.
3. What materials are you bringing to this building, by the way of character qualities or doctrinal teaching? Are you contributing imperishable values? None-genuine products of piety will be licked up by the flames.
4. Our building will be subjected to the scrutiny of fire when "the day" shall break in upon us. This "can only mean Christ's Judgment Day." It is "a supernatural, unprecedented day, dawning not like our mild familiar sunrise, but in splendour of judgment fire." *E.G.T.* Comp. Rom. 2:16; Acts 17:31; Matt. 25:19.
5. It is perilous to forget personal responsibility in this matter of building. Faithfulness will yield sweet rewards. Carelessness will invite the trying test of purging fire, not of purgatory, but of the judgment, when all that which is unsound, false and erroneous will simply be licked up by the flames, yet if the individual's own personal life is founded upon the rock he shall be saved.

II. *The Church as the temple of God.* vv. 16-17.
1. The Church is the place where God dwells on earth. Of old God dwelt by a visible symbol — the Shechinah — in the temple. So He is in the midst of His people. The Church is the peculiar residence of God. The Christian community is the consecrated dwelling place of God. To mar the beauty of this temple is inviting severe punishment as Ananias and Sapphira found out.

2. The Church is constituted as the temple of God by the indwelling of the Holy Spirit. The Church is the seat of the Holy Spirit's operations and influences, influences which produce appropriate effects.
3. To defile this temple is to work structural injury to the building and results in immoralities and divisions.
4. Whosoever thus desecrates the temple, "him will God destroy." That warning is sounded with an awful emphasis. Take heed. "The Lord is an avenger in all these things." I Tim. 4:6.

III. *The Church in relation to the world.* vv. 18-23.
1. She is not to allow the cleverness of the world to dictate her policies. Let us not be fascinated by mere cleverness. Mere talent is not enough. We need consecration. "When once idolatry of talent enters the Church, then farewell to spirituality." *Robertson.*
2. The Old Testament already teaches the lesson that those who lean merely upon intellectual and cultural accomplishments will suffer defeat. The passages cited are Job 5:13 and Psalm 94:11.
3. We are bidden to look past changing means and methods to the throne of God and draw our inspiration from there.
4. Christ who demands our subordination, supplies in Himself the grand example. *E.G.T.*

Conclusion:—

"The apostle has now vindicated God's rights in His Church and recalled the Corinthians from their carnal strife and pursuit of worldly wisdom to the unity, sanctity and grandeur of their Christian calling, which makes them servants of God through Christ, and in His right the heir of all things." *E.G.T.*

VII.

THE MINISTER'S PLACE BEFORE MAN AND GOD

I Cor. 4:1-21

Introduction:—

a) A recent writer presents a small list of ministerial qualities generally sought in the preacher. He is expected to be: a religious personality, a moral character, a quick thinker, a man of common sense, a man of prayer, a disciplined mind, of intellectual power, a model citizen, well-versed, sympathetic, resourceful, energetic, courageous, patient, peaceful, serious yet having a sense of humor, familiar with science and psychology, theologically and also politically minded, responding to local and universal interests.

b) Rather measure the man according to God's standards. Commissioned by God the preacher has: 1. *a definite task to perform:* to tell others what he has heard concerning Jesus Christ manifested in the flesh. I Tim. 2:7; II Tim. 1:11; II Tim. 4:2; Tit. 2:1; II Tim. 4:5. 2. *a definite burden to bear*, II Tim. 1:8; and 3. *a definite situation to face as "a good soldiers of Jesus Christ."* II Tim. 2:3. (So Karl Barth in an address on the "Ministry of the Word" given Sept. 11, 1934.)

c) This passage provides the minister with a looking glass which reflects reality.
I. *The Minister's Place is clearly defined.* vv. 1-5.
   1. He is a minister of Christ. v.1.
   2. He is a steward of the mysteries of God. v. 1.
   3. He is required to be faithful. v. 2.
   4. He is reassured as to the correctness of his ministry not by his conscience merely, but by his Lord. v. 3-4. "Since Paul accepted justification by faith in Christ, not his innocence, but his Saviour's merit has become his fixed ground of assurance." *E.G.T.*
   5. His place, as that of every one, will be determined not by the opinions of men, but by the Lord Himself at His coming. v. 5.
II. *The Minister's Place measures up to the Challenge of the World.* vv. 10-13.
   1. An estimate of the minister is not to go "beyond the things which are written." v. 6. The reign of the Word inspires true humility.
   2. It is presumptious and ungrateful to yield to egoistic boasting, when as a matter of fact God is the Bestower of every gift. v. 7.
   3. He will meet with spiritual satiety on the part of the hearers, but that is only a sign of arrested growth. They think they have already entered the promised kingdom. One could only wish that they had. v. 8. Comp. *E.G.T.*
   4. He is not the Greek gentleman given to luxury and waste, but beset on every hand by trying circumstances:

      a) doomed to death. v. 9.
      b) a spectacle unto the world. v. 9.
      c) fool's (for Christ's sake, to be sure) and disfranchised (cl. Gr.) while they are both wise and strong as seen by the world. v. 10. But "the Church is on dangerously good terms with the world." *E.G.T.*
      d) poverty, hardships, privations, ridicule, abuse, persecution, degradation await him constantly. vv. 11-13. Is he still to be envied?

III. *The Minister's Place is intended to be an office of spiritual admonishment.* vv. 14-21.
    1. This admonishing may be marked by sarcasm and severity, but it is motivated by love. v. 14.
    2. Nursery-governors there are indeed many, but few real guides. v. 15.
    3. Imitation is the law of the child's life. v. 16.
    4. Teaching and life must correspond, both are "in Christ." Paul's preaching has everywhere been corroborated by his habits of life. v. 17.
    5. Personal examination will reveal what is pretense and what is power. vv. 18-19.
    6. The Divine realm is not built up by windy words, but by power. Paul is ready to submit to the same test. II Cor. 13:1-10.
    7. Shall the correction be that of the rod or of love?

Conclusion:—

    Strain, hardship, conflict — these are the implications of the ministry. The ministry of the Word has its own discipline, overlooked by the world, yet severly real.

VIII.

MORAL EARNESTNESS

I Cor. 5:1-13.

Introduction:—

"The conflict undertaken by Christianity was one against sins of the flesh, such as fornication, adultery, and unnatural vices. . . . Everywhere you find the ethical demands occupying the front rank. . . . These Christian communities seek to regulate their common life by principles of the strictest morality, tolerating no unholy members in their midst, and well aware that with the admission of immorality their very existence ceases. The fearful punishment to which Paul sentences the incestuous person (I Cor. 5) is not exceptional." (Harnack, The Mission and Expansion of Christianity in the First Three Centuries, Engl. Translation I. p. 207.)

With Chapter V. begins the II. Division of the book, dealing with questions of social morals. The discussion turns to moral problems. Paganism enacted its toll from the church in Corinth by leading some to deflect from the purity of thought and practice demanded by the Gospel. The unbridled reign of natural impulses works devastation in the realm of the spiritual. One who allows himself to be ruled by these dark instincts becomes a detriment to the fellowship.

The underlying principle is the same however. This chapter stands in close relation to the previous discussion. One spirit manifests itself in all these things. These misconceptions that have led to spiritual pride work themselves out into social corruptions. The tenor of the message is the same throughout. Doctrinal and ethical expressions are governed by the same rule. The Gospel works a crisis in every domain of life. Goethe sensed this deeply as the classic passage from "Faust" indicates, but the inspired Apostle has a way out. Victory is available in the finished work of Calvary and in the power of His resurrection.

I. *The Case Calling For Correction.* vv. 1-2.
  1. The sin named. The description brands the sin as sin of unparalleled blackness. It was of such sort that even in heathen society it would be looked upon as an abomination. v. 1.
  2. The question asked: "What are you going to do about it?" v. 2.
     a) Will you still be puffed up? "Paul confronts the pride of the Corinthian Church with this crushing fact; no intellectual brilliance, no religious enthusiasm, can cover this hideous blot." *E.G.T.*
     b) The Church ought to put on funeral mourning — over "a brother dead to God, by sin, alas! undone." *E.G.T.*
     c) There should be action characterized by a high sense of spiritual responsibility. *(Praxas instead of Poiesas, E.G.T.)* Situations like these can not be tolerated. The Church must

take steps to correct this moral lapse. It is to be done not in the spirit of pharisaism, but in Christ-like sympathy with the fallen, and yet with all firmness, and the eager desire to make the Christian message effective. The Church will gain by including these elements promptly.

II. *The Apostle's Method of dealing with the case.* vv. 3-5.
 1. He is spiritually present to give his full attention to the case. v. 3.
 2. The doom of the culprit will be unquestionably pronounced by him, not as acting merely upon his own impulse, but as looking to the Head of the Church. vv. 3-4.
 3. Judgment will be pronounced "in the name of our Lord Jesus," as looking to Him as "a third Supreme Presence" and with the concurrent action of the church assembled. v. 4.
 4. The culprit will be delivered unto Satan. v. 5. Paul has apostolic authority to mete out this judgment and he will not delay the execution of sentence. This extreme action is necessary in order to bring the culprit to his senses. While extremely sorry because this name must be blotted out from the membership roll, yet the church acts from a high sense of responsibility toward her Lord and Master. The Church must be uncompromising. The membership must know that either "Christ is Lord of all, or He is not Lord at all."
 5. The delivering up unto Satan included excommunication as a spiritually remedial visitation of the

sinner and perhaps also a severe physical infliction. Comp. Ananias and Elymas. *E.G.T.*

III. *The Case calls for a Reassertion of the Christian Consciousness.* vv. 6-8.
  1. The old leaven of vice and sin permeated the Church as a body. There is no ground for pharisaic boasting, but rather for heart-searching examination. v. 6.
  2. "Our Passover hath been sacrificed—even Christ." v. 7. "Participation in the sacrifice of Christ presumes unleavenedness in the participants." *E.G.T.*
  3. "Let us keep the feast." The path from mourning to feasting lies in the fact of the newness of life in Christ and the power of His resurrection. Easter day is not to be kept as a feast merely, but as a constant demonstration of the fact and presence of resurrection victory within the Church. The minister who had his congregation sing an Easter hymn every Sunday was conscious of the relation of all of life to the message of the first Easter morning. Think of Augustine's conversion as the renewing force of this experience crashed into his life in the reading of Romans 13:11-14. Yes -- "The day is at hand," the day of victory in Christ's triumph. Look to Him and rejoice.

IV. *The Case calls for Immediate Action.* vv. 9-13.
  1. Do not hesitate to exercise discipline. v. 9.
  2. The matter is not settled by merely criticizing the world, or even by withdrawing from it. v. 10. For a setting forth of a Christian's relation to the world see John 17:14-19.

3. Do not subject yourself to corrupting influences. v. 11.
4. It is within the Church that these matters are to be settled. v. 12. The church is the place where these matters must be faced. The message of the risen Christ furnishes the criterion by which situations like these must be judged and handled. Christ's principles are determinative in all matters of belief and practice. "It is the spirit that giveth life; the flesh profiteth nothing: the words that I have spoken unto you are spirit, and are life" (John 6:63). This must direct the decision in matters as these.
4. "Purge away the wicked man from among yourselves." v. 13.

Conclusion:—

The Church cannot afford to side-step these issues. In so far as the transforming message of the resurrection fact is really dominant in the life of the group, situations as described here will be immediately and severly dealt with. Sensualism and saintliness can not march together under the same flag.

IX.
THE CHRISTIAN IN RELATION TO LAW AND THE NATURAL LIFE

I Cor. 6:1-20.

Introduction:—

Surrounded by paganism, the Corinthian Christians were again and again subjected to the tempting suggestiveness of heathen practices. But they must not forget the dignity of their high and holy calling. Our times make necessary again just such plain speaking on matters here broached.

While unhesitatingly tearing the mask from any ungenuine expression of the Christian life, Paul does not dwell upon negatives any longer than necessary. Ethical life receives its force and power from the fact that the Christian is conscious of the dignity of his calling and considers the cost of his redemption. "The saints shall judge the world." "Ye were bought with a price."

> Fight the fight, Christian,
> Jesus is o'er thee;
> Run the race, Christian,
> Heaven is before thee:
> He who hath promised
> Faltereth never;
> The love of eternity
> Flows on forever.

I. *The Sorry Spectacle of Un-Christian Litigation.* vv. 1-8.
  1. Think of the inconsistency of going outside the church in settling disputes. v. 1. The question reveals considerable feeling. "You treat the Church, the seat of the Holy Spirit (3:16f), as though it were without authority or wisdom; you take the case from the highest to the lowest!" *E.G.T.*
  2. Christians are qualified to settle disputes because of the dignity of their present and future position. vv. 2-3. Saints now, they shall sit in judgment over the world then . This accords with the words of Jesus. Matt. 19:28; Luke 22:30. Barnes suggests: "Perhaps the idea is, not that they shall then be qualified to see the justice of the condemnation which shall be passed on the wicked; they shall have a clear and distinct view of the case."
  3. Eschatology has practical bearing. Schlatter devotes a paragraph to point this out. He observes: "The Corinthian Christians dwell much on eschatological matters, but the will is not influenced by these considerations. If the Corinthians really believed that some day they would judge the world, they would be more serious in the exercise of legal matters. Paul combats an eschatology which remains simply an idea and does not become a real hope to give direction to the will."
  4. Why does the Church draw the strength out of its own resources to settle such disputes concerning "mine" and "thine"? v. 4. Why must "the less esteemed" (Auth. Vers.), those "who are of

no account in the church" (Rev. Vers.) be called in? Why must heathen magistrates, in whose virtue, piety and qualifications for just judgment Christians could have little confidence, be called in? This is a question of indignation and so construed by Barnes and Schlatter. Others render the verse in tthe imperative, so that the "less esteemed" are the inferior members within the Church, but according to Schlatter such differentiation between more and less worthy in the Church, is entirely un-Pauline.

5. Why does not the Church produce able judges? v. 5. Can a church so poverty stricken with real men, still boast of superior wisdom?

6. Law-suits between Christians should not be at all necessary. They ought to take wrong rather. Certainly should there be no necessity to appeal to civil magistrates. vv. 6-8.

Are law-suits ever proper? Barnes affirms in the following cases:

1. As an amicable suit, to determine what the law is.
2. When differences occur between Christians and men of the world, who do not recognize the place of the Church.
3. Where a Christian is injured in his person, character, or property, he has a right to seek redress.

II. *The Purifying Power of Christian Allegiance.* vv. 9-11.

1. "Wrong-doers will not inherit God's kingdom"

(which neverthelss they profess to seek, 1:7ff) — an axiom of revelation, indeed of conscience, but the over-clever sometimes forget elementary moral principles." *E.G.T.*
2. The church must be purged of all libertinism. But whatever the church does in the matter, these ten classes of sinners and those like them will be excluded from the kingdom. vv. 9-10.
3. Three verbs "washed," "sanctified," "justified," indicate the process by which Christians enter the kingdom. v. 11. Very emphatic is the last phrase, which makes it quite definite that the action implied is "of our God." The "but" of v. 11 is very emphatic. The contrast between the *"some"* and the *"ye"* is sharply accentuated. The order of words does not justify a construction contrary to Paul's emphasis, which usually puts justification first. "This verse brings in the whole subject of redemption, and states in most emphatic manner the various stages by which the sinner is saved, and by this single passage, a man may obtain all the essential knowledge of the plan of salvation." *Barnes*.

III. *The Christian Warfare against Libertinism and Licentiousness.* vv. 12-20.
1. The cry of uncontrolled libertinism: "All is lawful." v. 12.
2. The answer of Christian restraint: "not all things are expedient" — they do not profit, but are injurious and hurtful.
3. The seductiveness of evil is to be met with grim

determination: "I will not be brought under the power of any." v. 12. A Christian ought to be firm in purpose "not to be slave of habit, not to be subdued by any practice that might corrupt his mind, fetter his energies, or destroy his freedom as a man and as a Christian." *Barnes*.

4. We are not to yield to the proverbial appeal to satisfy the baser appetites. Our Christian hope extends also over the functions of the body. vv. 13-14. To the Christian life means much more than the satisfying of the appetites or gratification of sensual pleasures. In these matters too, belief and hope in the resurrection determine the point of view. The body is to share in the promise of eternal persistence. Unchastity and intemperance reduce man to the animal state. How shameful such behavior that looks upon life as a continued carnival! The Christian hope will exert a controlling discipline over all bodily functions.

5. In order not to fall into this regrettable lapse we need to remind ourselves constantly of our intimate union with Christ. We ought to be thoroughly abhorent to the idea of corrupting this union to form one that links us to the body of pollution. How emphatic this outcry: "God forbid." vv. 15-17. The Christian's body stands in closest relations to the organism called the Church. Its functions are to honor, not dishonor, Christ Who is the recognized Head of the Christian fellowship. Union with Christ is the first requisite of holy living.

6. We have this solemn command: "flee fornication."

Do not stay to reason or debate, retreat and win the victory. v. 18.
7. "To praise God with our body and with our spirit is the purpose of our existence." (vv. 19-20) *Barth.*

Conclusion:—

To follow Christ calls for self-denial. Paul is insistent that all of life shall move in that direction. The body as well as the soul is to live out the divine purposes of God. A Christian takes God into account in all his affairs. He moves in the presence of His risen Lord.

X.

SHOULD ONE MARRY?

I Cor. 7:1-40.

Introduction:—
"Christian love makes all life one great duty."
"There are two rocks in this world of ours on which the soul must either anchor or be wrecked. The one is God; the other is the sex opposite to itself. The one is the "Rock of Ages" on which if the human soul anchors it lives the blessed life of faith; against which if the soul be dashed and broken, there ensues the wreck of Atheism — the worst ruin of the soul. The other rock is of another character. Blessed is the man, blessed is the woman, whose life-experience has taught a confiding belief in the excellences of the sex opposite to their own—a blessedness second only to the blessedness of salvation. And the ruin in the other case is second only to the ruin of everlasting perdition — the same wreck and ruin of the soul." *Fredk. W. Robertson.*

This chapter stands related to the contents of the Epistle as such in a twofold way:
    a) as forming a part of the second division dealing with questions of social morals. See Introd. to V.
    b) This chapter begins the series of topics mentioned in the letter of the Corinthians to Paul, to which

the apostle answers introducing his remarks by the phrase: "Now concerning the things whereof ye wrote." Schlatter includes in these topics 7:1; 7:25; 8:1; 12:1; 16:1; 16:12. (p. 208).

This chapter connects with that which immediately precedes by continuing the discussion on the crisis produced in the natural life as confronted by Christ.

I. *Marriage is ordained of God and to be kept sacred.* vv. 1-9.
   1. The forbidding note of v. 1 is to be read in the light of
      a) the Corinthian conditions which favored unchecked sensuality.
      b) the fuller and more idealistic teaching of the Apostle, which can be found in other epistles. See Eph. V.

      The instructions given here bear the marks of local impress and temporary aim while otherwise Paul reveals a very exalted sense of the spiritual import of marriage.
   2. Christian marriage is to be between one man and one woman. Celibacy does not improve the spiritual life. Think of the evils that have grown out of the monastic system and the celibacy of the clergy forbidden to marry. Comp. Barnes.
   3. Husband and wife belong together in person, property, and in every respect. vv. 3-4. The equal rights of man and woman are maintained.
   4. Married persons are to co-operate to keep the spiritual ideal uppermost; unitedly they are to op-

pose Satanic perversions of the marriage ideal. v. 5.
5. Each is to cultivate the charisma of God. v. 6-7. God bestows gifts to be practically employed.
6. It is better to marry, even in times of distress and persecution, than to fall prey to raging and consuming passions. vv. 8-9.

II. *Marriage is not to be dissolved by divorce.* vv. 10-16.
1. In this matter Paul puts himself under the authority of Christ. v. 1. "He cites Christ's words in distinction from his own (12), not as though his word was insufficient (see, to the contrary, 40; 2:16; 5:3f; 14:37 etc.), but inasmuch as this was the principle upon which the Lord had pronounced categorically." *E.G.T.* Comp. Matt. 19:1-12.
2. Mixed marriages come under the same Christian regulations. vv. 12-13. "The Christian spouse is forbidden to cast off the non-Christian in terms identical for husband and wife. Man and woman stand on equal footing in this matter." *E.G.T.*
3. The Christian family is a solidarity in the blessings of which the children also participate. v. 14. This text "enunciates the principle which leads to Infant Baptism, viz. that the child of Christian parents shall be treated as a Christian." *E.G.T.* quoting Lightfoot.
4. If there is divorce (on the grounds of adultery or wilful desertion), there is to be no re-marriage. v. 11; v. 15.
5. The salvation of husband or wife should be the foremost object of marriage. v. 16.

III. *Marriage is to be lived out on Christian principles, as also every other calling of life.* vv. 17-24.

Like Marriage every calling of life calls for the incorporation of the spirit of Christ.

1. Let everyone, whether single or married be content with his present state. v. 17.
2. We are to be more concerned with the commandments of God than with the matter of our outward state. God demands not outer observance, but the heart primarily. vv. 18-19. Compare Gal. 5:6; 6:15.
3. Let nothing be allowed to undermine the basis of our call: for salvation is by grace and through faith. Comp. Gal. 2:11-21; 3:2f; 5:2-6. "Abide" means to stand fast. v. 20.
4. We are Christ's bondservants regardless of our social status. vv. 21-24.

IV. *Marriage of virgins and widows deserves special considerations.* vv. 25-40.

1. As to the place of marriagable daughters in this matter Paul has no command, but an opinion, but note: "The distinction made is not between higher and lower grades of inspiration or authority, but between *peremptory rule* and *conditional advice* requiring the concurrence of those advised." *E.G.T.* Paul's opinion, as much as his injunction, is that of the Lord's steward and mouthpiece. v. 25.
2. It is good not to effect any change in critical times. v. 26.
3. One entering the married state must reckon with the fact that it incurs obligations and frequently

invites additional burdens. vv. 27-28.
4. It is well to face all situations of life with a certain spiritual detachment. vv. 29-31. Prepare to cut loose from the shore of time. "The fashion of this world passeth away." v. 31.
5. Marriage is beset with matters of passing interest. vv. 32-34.
6. After all, virgins are free to marry, provided marriage is contracted upon an honorable basis and not in conflict with existing conditions. vv. 35-38.
7. A widow is free to marry again, provided such marriage is contracted "in the Lord," but "she is happier if she abide as she is." vv. 39-40. That's plain enough.

Conclusion:—

In all these matters the Christian is not simply to follow his own personal inclinations. Worldly motives must be set aside by one who lives and walks "in the Lord." The Christian seeks the constant guidance of the Spirit. To him the goal of all of life is the glory of God.

XI.

KNOWLEDGE IN RELATION TO CHRISTIAN CONDUCT

I Cor. 8:1-13

Introduction:—
- a) The argument of this chapter is offered to meet a practical situation: Would a Christian be permitted to eat meat slaughtered for pagan sacrificial purposes and subsequently sold in the public market?
- b) This chapter is part of the section (VIII-X) which confronts the Church with the fact that petty questions of conscience and conduct must give way to abiding principles developed by living expressions of faith, hope, and love.
- c) We must see to it that the working leaven of the Gospel is kept fresh by looking past accidental forms of social expression to the ringing truths that turn heart and mind in the direction of enlightened and consecrated relationship to Christ as the Lord of life.

I. *Knowledge needs to be corrected by love.* vv. 1-3.
  1. Note the close similarity of the style of Paul and John by comparing this chapter to I John 4. The contents turn upon the same major key: knowledge is good, but it must find practical direction in the exercise of love toward God and man.

2. A little knowledge is a dangerous thing. Knowledge is too apt to become pretension unless corrected by the claim of love. Intellectualism is not a safe guide to conduct.
3. Pride of knowledge was the greatest danger to the Corinthian church, as revealed also by the first four chapters. There it led to spiritual sins, here to practical perversion of conduct.
4. "Knowledge operating alone makes it an engine of destruction." *E.G.T.*
5. Love is constructive, edifying. Comp. Eph. 4:15f; Matt. 22:37-40; I John 4:16-21. "The great theme of ch. 13 appears here for the first time." *Barth.*
6. "Loveless knowledge is self-stultifying." *E.G.T.* v. 2. "Prefer to seem to know nothing; and if to any thou shouldst seem to be somebody, distrust thyself." *Epictetus.*
7. "Our love is the reflex of the divine love and knowledge directed toward us." *E.G.T.* v. 3. Do not miss the rich thought of this verse. How much greater divine grace than human logic! Descartes says, "I think therefore I am." Paul writes, I am known of God and thus I am grounded in His love and I have my existence in His grace. What wonderful depth of divine disclosure and condescension to contemplate!

II. *Knowledge needs to be related to great doctrinal realities.* vv. 4-6.
1. The tenor and solemn rhythm of the words suggest a confessional formula, a *confessio fidei* as in I John 5:18ff.

2. Polytheism exerts a fascinating power. v. 5. "Polytheism is man's attempt to rid himself of the notion of responsibility to one moral Lawgiver and Judge by dividing up his manifestations, and attributing them to separate wills." (Strong, Systematic Theology, p. 125.)
3. The Christian Church affirms positively her belief in the unity of God and the Lordship of Jesus Christ. v. 6. "The universe is of God through Christ (Heb. 1:2; John 1:3); we are for God through Christ (II Cor. 5:18; Eph. 1:5)" *E.G.T.* This verse speaks to the deepest interests of Christian thinking. It approaches unto a confessional statement. The question concerning the origin of things finds its answer in the phrase "of whom." The fact of the Lordship of Christ finds expression in the terse statement *"through* whom are all things, and we through him." "The faith which refers all things to the one God our Father as their spring, and subordinates all things to the one Lord our Redeemer, leaves no smallest spot in the universe for other deities." *E.G.T.*

III. *Knowledge needs to be supplemented by practical considerations.* vv. 7-10.
1. Matters of conscience are determined by clarity of faith. v. 7.
2. Neither over-indulgence nor abstinence will commend us to God. v. 8.
3. We need to exercise care for the sake of the weaker brother. vv. 9-10.

IV. *Knowledge needs to take on a Christo-centric form.* vv. 11-13.

1. Remember Christ died for the weak as for the strong. v. 11. Beware lest Christ's death is frustrated of its dear object through heartless folly. "The principle of union with Christ, which forbids sin against oneself (6:15), forbids sin against one's brother." *E.G.T.*
2. To offend the weaker brother is to offend Christ. v. 12. "To destroy their souls is to pain His heart and to injure His cause." *Barnes.* Comp. Matt. 10:40; Luke 10:16.
3. Have the brother in mind (mentioned four times in these verses) and let love to him control knowledge.

Conclusion:—

a) Note the doctrinal side of the argument of this chapter. Christian thought leaves no room for idols. To maintain a place in the Christian fellowship idolatry of whatever form and kind must be overcome. The Church can only live and thrive as she keeps her faith in the triune God pure and untainted by idolatry.

b) The practical side of the argument is well stated by Barnes: "If all Christians had Paul's delicate sensibilities and Paul's strength of Christian virtue, and Paul's willingness to deny himself to benefit others, the aspect of the Christian world would soon change." (Notes ad loc.)

XII.

SELF-DENIAL PRACTICALLY DEMONSTRATED

I Cor. 9:1-27.

Introduction:—
- a) This interim discussion dealing with the justification of apostolic freedom, is nevertheless part of the argument advanced in the preceding chapter. Paul means to furnish here a practical example of the secret origin and open effectiveness of self-mastery. "The whole chapter is an incidental discussion, of the subject of his apostleship in illustration of the sentiment advanced in ch. 8:13, that he was willing to practice self-denial for the good of others; and is one of the most elevated, heavenly and beautiful discussions in the New Testament, and contains one of the most enobling descriptions of the virtue of self-denial, and of the principles which should actuate the Christian ministry, anywhere to be found. All classic writings would be searched in vain, and all records of profane history, for an instance of such pure and elevated principle as is presented in this chapter." *Barnes.*
- b) The apostle's declaration of freedom finds pungent expression in the principle voiced by Luther: 1. "Christ's man is a free master in all things and in subjection to no one." 2. "Christ's man is the servant of everyone and subject to everybody."

c) Self-mastery has temporal and an eternal aspect. We practice it to succeed now, and to gain the crown then.

I. *The hidden forces of a life of self-denial.* vv. 1-3.

As personified in the apostle this means:

1. His life reflects the personal experience of meeting with the living Christ. v. 1. He insists that this experience is more than spiritual apprehension of the fact of Christ, more than an ecstatic vision. He means that it is nothing less than "that actual beholding of the human and glorified Redeemer which befell him on the way to Damascus." *E.G.T.* --

   The Damascus road experience is still basic in the equipment of the minister of Christ. Turn to Wm. Stidger's book: "Men of the Great Redemption." (Cokesbury Press, 1931.)

2. The Master has approved his work by affixing his seal thereto. v. 2. "The Corinthian Church was a shining evidence of Paul's commission." *E.G.T.*

3. The very nature of his ministry is his *"apologia pro vita."* v. 3.

II. *The Apostle's bill of rights.* vv. 4-6.

1. He claims the right to adequate material support. v. 4.

2. He claims the right of the ordinary comforts of married life. v. 5.

   See how far Paul is from justifying enforced celibacy. Neither is there in this passage any suggestion in defense of the scandalous prac-

tice of priests' and monks' keeping of "sisters."
E.G.T.
3. He claims the right, if the situation so demands it, and the interests of his ministry require it, to be exempt from manual labor. v. 6.

III. *The Christian ministry generally is entitled to similar rights.* vv. 7-14.

A five-fold proof is presented:
1. On the grounds of natural analogy. v. 7. This rule of providing material support for service rendered obtains in the soldier's camp, Luke 11: 21f; in the tending of the vineyard, Matt. 20:1ff; 21:28ff; in the care of the flock. John 10 and 21:15.
2. Scripture proof. vv. 8-10. "The right of Christ's ministers to eat and drink is safeguarded by the principle that gives the ox his provender out of the corn he treads." *E.G.T.*
3. There is proof in the intrinsic justice of the matter. v. 11. The high and holy things imparted certainly merit temporal sustenance.
4. The claim to this right is justified by reference to the temple service. v. 13. Comp. Lev. 6:8-7:38 and Num. 18:8-19.
5. We have the express commandment of the Lord. v. 14. The Lord has appointed that those who preach the good tidings are to live of the good tidings. Matt. 10:10; Luke 10:8.

IV. *The service of self-denial as practiced by the Apostle.* vv. 15-23.

1. He will not be put into pecuniary dependence. v. 15.
2. He works under compulsion of Sovereign Grace. v. 16. How gloriously he demonstrates "the expulsive power of a new affection."
3. He knows himself entrusted with a sacred trust. v. 17. "In Paul's consciousness of stewardship there mingled submission to God, gratitude for the trust bestowed, and independence of human control." *E.G.T.*
4. He will have his reward "the satisfaction felt by a generous mind in rendering unpaid service." v. 18. "He repudiates reward in the mercenary sense, to claim it in the larger ethical sense." *E.G.T.*
5. He will free himself from everybody, just that he might be everybody's servant. v. 19.
6. He identifies himself with every class of people, vv. 20-22, not in unchristian compliance with men, but as motivated by the practical wisdom of true Christian love and self-denial in the exercise of his office. *E.G.T.*

V. *The runner in the race has his eye upon the crown.* vv. 24-27.
1. Victory can not be had without self-mastery.
2. "Do not be satisfied with running, but make sure of winning." *E.G.T.* v. 24.
3. Self-indulgence will bring failure to the attempt of winning the coveted prize. v. 25.
4. Self-discipline is the secret to attainment. vv. 26-27.

Conclusion:—

> Awake, my soul, stretch every nerve,
> And press with vigor on;
> A heavenly race demands thy zeal,
> And an immortal crown.
>
> Blest Saviour, introduced by Thee,
> Have I my race begun;
> And, crowned with victory, at Thy feet
> I'll lay my honors down.
>
> *Philip Doddridge.*

XIII.

IDOLATRY IN THE LIGHT OF HISTORY
AND
CONTEMPORARY CHURCH CUSTOMS

I Cor. 10:1-33.

Introduction:—

The fear of reprobation just mentioned (9:27) is no idle talk, but the history of the O. T. church presents a warning example. If the Christians at Corinth yield to idolatrous practices they will fare no better than the people of Israel in the wilderness.

The tenth chapter is obviously connected with 9:27. Paul disciplined himself lest he became a castaway. "This very word brought the subject into a more serious light, and the idea contained in it is the hinge on which the chapter turns." (Robertson).

Occasioned by treacherous temptations of idolatry making inroads upon every domain of life, the multifarious warning of the Apostle never swerves from the main theme: the glory of God. v. 31. "Man's chief end is to glorify God, and to enjoy him for ever." Westm. Shorter Catechism.

I. *The privileges Israel enjoyed. vv. 1-5.*

    1. Israel's history furnishes instructive material of use to the church then and always. We ought to welcome the information provided. v. 1 a.

    2. The parrallel of Israel and the church approaches identification. v. 1 b. "Our fathers" identifies the

N. T. church with Israel." E.G.T. See also: Rom. 4:1.11ff; 11:17f; Gal. 3:7.29.
3. "All" repeated five times gives point to the warning. "Even those who were destroyed had this privilege." Barnes
4. Israel enjoyed the guidance and protection of the cloud. v. 1.
5. Israel looked back upon the great deliverance at the Red Sea. v. 1.
6. As the Israelites were baptized unto Moses, so Christians are baptized unto Christ. The Corinthians are committed to the guidance of Christ. v. 2.
7. Delivered in a miraculous way, Israel also received sustenance in a supernatural manner. vv. 3-4.
8. It was "spiritual" food and drink that sustained Israel. That phrase does not deny the materiality of the provisions, but simply implies that these gifts had spiritual meaning and influence. *E.G.T.* It is called spiritual to denote "its purity, value and excellence." Barnes
9. They drank of a spiritual rock "that followed them," v. 4. We are to remember here the incidents of Rephidim (Tx. 17) and Kadesh (Num. 20). To take the following of the rock literally would be to accept the old rabbinical legend. "We must not disgrace Paul by making him say that the incarnate Christ followed the march of Israel in the shape of a lump of rock." *E.G.T.* quoting Hf.
10. "The rock was Christ." v. 4. b. Christ was spiritually present with the O. T. church and the grace attending his ordinances was mediated by Him.

By all this Paul meant to intimate: "The Jews had as full privileges as you Corinthians have, and yet they fell; you have your privileges, but you may see in these examples that privileges are no cause for security, but only for greater heed." *F. W. Robertson.*

II. *The sins Israel committed.* vv. 6-14.
1. The experiences of the Israelites are types furnishing us a warning that we do not sin in the same way. v. 6.
2. The general admonition is specialized in four particulars:
    a) against idolatry, which Israel practiced in connection will the worship of the golden calf. Ex. 32. Wild, careless merriment will destroy spiritual life.
    b) against fornication. v. 8. The reference is to the licentious intercourse with the daughters of Moab. Num. 25:1-9. Here 23,000 instead of 24,000 in Num. The first fell by the hand of God, the others by the judges. This is the solution offered by Barnes.
    c) against tempting the Lord. v. 9.
    "The sins condemned in vv. 7-8 are sins of *sensuality;* these, of unbelief—which takes two forms: of *presumption,* daring God's judgments; or of *despair,* doubting His goodness. The whole wilderness history, with its crucial events of Massah and Meribah, is represented as a trying of the Lord. Psalm 95:8 f. Num. 14:22." *E.G.T.*
    d) against murmuring. v. 10. "Paul alludes specifically to the rebellion of Korah and its pun-

ishment—the only instance of violent death overtaking this sin (Num. 16:41)." *E.G.T.*
3. The lessons of these judgments provide admonitions for all succeeding generations. This manner of divine administrations holds good until the end of times. v. 11.
4. Confidence in our own security is no evidence that we are safe. v. 12.
5. To the despondent there is held out the encouragement that "God is faithful." vv. 12-13. "For the natural trial a supernatural providence guarantees sufficient aid." *E.G.T.* "God's faithfulness alone is a match for the force of temptation." *Barth.*
6. v. 14 gives the final point to all that has been urged. "All these considerations combine to enforce the appeal, Flee from idolatry." *E.G.T.*

III. *Contrasting the communion of the Lord and the communion of demons.* vv. 15-22.

1. Appeal to the intelligence of the readers. v. 15.
2. Communion (koinonia) is the key-word of this passage. The Lord's Supper constitutes a communion, centering in Christ. Idolatrous practices lead to a communion with demons as the unseen objects of idolatrous worship.
3. Christians partake of the "blessed cup." v. 16. "Christ blessed this cup, making it thus for ever a cup of blessing." *E.G.T.* Other interpretations "the cup which gives blessing," Hebr. form: "the cup over which we pronounce blessings." The cup is blessed and so set apart for sacred use.
4. "The bread" is blessed equally with the cup. The symbolical act is that of breaking, as indicating the distribution to many of the one loaf.

5. The stress lies on "tou Christou," of Christ. Believers participate in Christ's complete redemption wrought through his bodily life and death and resurrection.
6. The fellowship of the Lord's table is vital to the Church. v. 17.
7. Israel enjoyed this festal communion in the Passover meal. v. 18.
8. The attendance upon the Lord's supper carries with it a prohibition of attendance at idol feasts. vv. 19-20. The gracious invitation to the communion table carries with it the responsibility of choice. Communion means entire commitment to Christ. Divided loyalty makes the benefits null and void. To enter into communion with Christ — opposed forces and devil-inspired minds will call out the devouring zeal of the Lord.
9. "Ye cannot." The forbidding tone is full of earnestness of warning and anxious solicitation in order that the purity of relationship to Christ shall be maintained. Allegiance to Christ will not permit this fraternizing with those in reality, arrayed against Him. The coming to the communion calls for a discerning of the spirits.
10. Coquetting will idolatry invites Christ's sovereign displeasure and such double-dealing brings peril and judgment. v. 22.

IV. *Christian liberty is governed by the principle of living to the glory of God.* vv. 23-33.

1. Communion and love of the brethren serve as guards of Christian liberty. vv. 23-24.
2. A concrete situation had best be understood in the light of the Lord's original ownership. vv. 25-26.

Cit. Psalm 24:1. "Consecration to an idol cannot deprive the Lord of anything." *E.G.T.*
3. Exercise freedom, yet regard the conscience of others. vv. 27-29.
4. vv. 31-32 conclude the matter with two solemn, comprehensive rules.
5. Through his own pattern Paul points the readers to that of his Master and theirs. v. 32. *E.G.T.* He speaks solely and entirely in the interest of preserving the Church and exalting the Head of the Church.

Conclusion:—

Remember that God is sovereign in all things. Seek the honor of Christ. Live on freely and trustfully, but remember that you belong to the fellowship of the Church, that you are governed by the all comprehending principle of seeking the glory of God and seek not only your own salvation, but that also of others.

XIV.

DECORUM AT CHURCH AND AT THE COMMUNION TABLE

I Cor. 11:1-34.

Introduction:—

In this chapter the Apostle returns to the internal affairs of the church to which he gave attention in Div. I. of the Epistle. Some of the topics considered there reappear here in a new connection: e. g. relationship of the sexes, (V.VI.AI.), the Lord's Supper (X.XI.), and the superiority of love to knowledge (VI).

At first sight, first and second part of this chapter seem to stand wide apart, but a closer examination will disclose the unity and the common thought underlying both main sections (vv. 1-16. and vv. 17-33). "We are dealing with a repudiation of a powerfully flourishing type of man in the Corinthian Church, with his tendency to wilful and self-seeking assertion of his influence. It is that which connects the two halves of the chapter."

It is clear from the Apostle's own argument that some of the references to contemporary culture and civilization have little meaning for our day, but in so far as they illustrate abiding principles they deserve attention, for thus they speak to conditions in the Church at the present time.

I. *The principle of the headship is determinative in minute matters.* vv. 1-6.

PREACHING CHRIST IN CORINTH

1. We may ignore the first verse as belonging to the preceding chapter. "It has been improperly separated from that chapter, and in reading should be read in connection with it." *Barnes.*
2. The Apostle commends his readers for their disposition to regard his authority and for their readiness of adherence to the ordinances (rather than traditions) in which they were instructed. v. 2.
3. This commendation however is not to weaken the censure which he needs to inflict. v. 3 a.
4. The first main point leaps into prominence. v. 3. "The indecorum in question offends against a foundation principle, viz. that of *subordination under the Divine government.*" *E.G.T.* "The question is one that touches the fundamental propieties of life (8-15); and the three headships enumerated belong to the hierarchy of nature." *E.G.T.* We are to remember that we stand within the Christian fellowship. The principle of subordination insisted upon finds its best defense in the fact that its specific reference is to conditions prevailing in the spiritual organism. In the spiritual sphere of the Christian life, as Gal. 3:28 indicates man and woman stand on a place of ideal quality. But just as other differences, such as rank and class, continue under the Christian regime, so this subordination is not done away with. The divine order is being maintained because it is designed in reference to Christ. The principle of headship, instead of burdening anyone, serves to vouchsafe to every individual his station and dignity, because it finds its crowning expression in the headship of Christ.

5. "The high doctrine just asserted applied to the matter of feminine attire." *E.G.T.* on vv. 4-g. Man must not be veiled. He has no head but Christ. It would be dishonoring Christ if a man would so forget himself as to deny his own position and masquerade as a woman.
6. The unveiled woman thereby expresses rebellion against the order and carrying this neglect of manners further still, she comes dangerously near to be classified with the heathen priestesses, who had surrendered to immorality. v. 6. "Physical barefacedness led to the inference of moral, in a city like Corinth."

II. *The place of man and woman before the Lord.* vv. 7-16.
1. "11:7-10 is a variation of the fundamental idea of 11:3: A man is to assert his manhood as the created image of God, as God's reflection upon earth, first created, not for the sake of woman." *Barth, op. cit.*
2. Each (man or woman) fills a place appointed in due subordination of rank and the apparel and attire is expressive of this. v. 7.
3. In both cases the appointed order goes back to the creation. vv. 8-9. "Woman originates *from* and was created *for* man, not vice versa." *E.G.T.*
4. "v. 10 is the counterstatement to v. 1 a, undeveloped there: For this reason the woman is bound to wear authority upon her head, for the reason stated in vv. 7 b.-9, that her nature is derived and auxiliary. *T.G.T.*
5. The last phrase of v. 10 "because of the angels" is a veritable crux to commentators. The explana-

tion of E.G.T. is acceptable: The angels are interested spectators of the conduct of Christian servants. The angels are present in Divine worship and are offended by irreverence and misconduct. Barnes advances virtually the same meaning and illustrates his point by reference tto Persian ladies.
6. "Man and woman are necessary each to the other and derive alike from God," remarks E.G.T. of v. 11 and quotes Tennyson: "Either sex alone is half itself . . . each fulfils defect in each, and always thought in thought, purpose in purpose, will in will they grow . . . the two-celled heart beating, with one full stroke, life."
7. The further appeal is to natural feeling. vv. 13-15.
8. "v. 16 closes the discussion sharply, with its appeal to established Christian rule." *E.G.T.*
9. The Word of God is to be represented in every domain of life. The sovereignty of God relates to every phase of it. The natural subordinations of life are not meant to be burdensome. Their proper observance reflects regard for the majesty of God. Contentions will be silenced where the simple rules of God are adhered to, and where His word is believed in as expressing His holy purpose and His great concern for man.

III. *Proper worship calls for orderly procedure.* vv. 17- 22.

1. The Apostle, ready to recognize any existing good, will not condone irregularity of worship. v. 17.
2. Divisions and factions stand in the way of the true purposefulness and exercise of the Christian fellowship. v 18-19.
3. This spirit of self-complacency and rebellion to

order is especially intolerable when it attempts to infringe upon the sacredness of the Communion service. vv. 20121.

4. Such perversion of the design of the Lord's supper merits severe rebuke. v. 22.

IV. *The Origin and Meaning of the Lord's Supper calls for reverent handling of the elements.* vv. 23-33.

1. The language employed suggests a graphic description of the night of nights when the supper was instituted. v.23. We have reason to shudder at the possibility that offense against the sacredness of this observance will perpetuate forever the darkness of the night in which Jesus was betrayed. The admonition to seek our salvation with fear and trembling is surely in place here. Narrow is the gate, and straitened the way, that leadeth unto life. Matt. 7:14.

2. In celebrating the ordinance enter into the meaning of bread and cup offered. vv. 24-25.

3. The meaning of Christ's death is to be vividly before us as we partake of these elements. By it we are to keep the memory of the atoning passion of the Saviour alive. v. 25.

4. The rite looks *forward* (until He come) as well as backward. v. 26.

5. Forgetting where we ought to be remembering dishonours this service.

6. The Lord's supper confronts us with searching scrutiny. It calls for serious self-examination.

7. Low spiritual conditions are not the least responsible for physical afflictions. v. 30.

8. Such chastening has its purpose. vv. 31-32.

Conclusion:—

"Religious decorum depends on two conditions—*a becoming spirit* associated with *fitting enternal arrangements*, such as good sense and reverence dictate." *E.G.T.*

XV.

THE *E PLURIBUS UNUM* OF SPIRITUAL ENDOWMENTS

I Cor. 12:1-31.

Introduction:—

In this chapter the Apostle gives the plea for the deepening of the inner life of the Church additional emphasis. While insisting on propriety in every phase of Church life, he now discloses the secret of such purifying and sustaining power. Vital church life is not attained through unbridled activity of man's spirit, but solely through the manifestation, operation and influence of the Holy Spirit.

As in 7:1 and 8:1 the Apostle is striking here a major theme elicited undoubtedly by the inquiry of the Corinthian church. The subject is today as timely as ever. "The Church of today is the same as in the day of the apostles. The life lived then is the life that animates it now... The wonderful and glorious revelation received by the Church of the first century was given, through it, to the Church of all ages, and is still effectual. And all the spiritual strength and insight, the inward grace, the clearer consciousness, received during the course of the ages are not lost, but form an accumulated treasure, increasing still by the ever-renewed additions of spiritual gifts." Kuyper, "The Work of the Holy Spirit."

I. *The criterion of the spirit's character.* vv. 1-3.

1. The subject of spiritual gifts is important for the Church at all times. Interest in them is justified and should be met by candid examination. v. 1 a.
2. It is of such importance also that it demands special care and particular attention. v. 1 b.
3. Christians are to distinguish clearly between the oracle and the voice of the Spirit. v. 2. Idols could never endow with such spiritual privileges as the Corinthians at present enjoyed.
4. Loyalty to Jesus Christ is the criterion. v. 3. The Holy Spirit will always honor Jesus Christ and will prompt all who are under his influence to love and reverence His name.
5. A spirit that calls Jesus accursed (anathema-vowed to God for destruction as under his curse) cannot be of God. v. 3. In bitter enmity the High Priest and the Jewish people so derided Jesus (Jn. 11:49), and the shout might be taken up by the priests and priestesses of the pagan gods. Surely the Corinthians will detect this malicious attack of the evil spirits.
6. While pretenders to inspiration only dishonor Christ, believers are led by the Holy Spirit to call Christ their Lord. v. 3. The recognition of Jesus as Lord certificates all true Christians as possessors of the Holy Spirit. The Spirit inspires believers to confess the Name of Christ. They express their allegiance to Him not in mystical, meaningless phrases, but by a clear, intelligent confession. Jesus is Lord is the watchword of those contending for the truth.

II. *The release of spiritual energies.* vv. 4-11.
  1. The operation of the one Spirit works wonderful diversity and fulness and bears a multiform fruit.

Members of the body of Christ may constantly replenish their energies by drawing upon the Spirit's inexhaustible store of gifts. vv. 4-6.
2. A Trinitarian Deity is active in a Trinitarian way. vv. 4-6. A Trinity of blessings—gifts, ministrations, workings—associates their possessors with a trinity of persons—Spirit, Lord, and God.
3. Each member has a personal gift by which he shows forth the Spirit. v. 7.
4. vv. 8-10 exhibit by way of example nine chief manifestations:—
   (1) wisdom:—large acquisition of truth .
   (2) knowledge: — truth intellectually apprehended: "deep insight into the mysteries of the kingdom." *Kuyper.*
   (3) faith:—in its energetic and heroic demonstration.
   (4) gifts of healing:—Mark 16:18. Are these dormant at present or is this endowment expressed in our time through the work of medical missions?
   (5) miracles:—"Their function confined them to distinctively the Apostolic Church, and they necessarily passed away with it." Warfield, Counterfeit Miracles, p. 6.
   (6) prophecy:—edifying gifts of speech.
   (7) discerning of spirits:—detecting errors and imposture.
   (8) kinds of tongues:—Acts 2:4. 7-11.
   (9) interpretation of tongues: — "evidently a faculty different from the power of speaking a foreign language; and yet it might be equally useful." *Barnes' Notes.*

5. There is unity in this rich variety of gifts and the sanctity of each is to be respected. v. 11.

III. *The unity of the body. vv. 12-19.*
1. The one Spirit suggests the similitude of "the body" for the Church. While a plastic figure here, in Ephesians and Colossians this expression becomes a fixed title. *E.G.T.*
2. Members of the church form a single body because by baptism they are placed under the ruling influence of the One Spirit. vv. 13-14.
3. The entire body suffers if a single organ refuses to function in relation to the whole. vv. 15-16.
4. One part cannot presume to stand for the whole. v. 17.
5. Every member of the body is under Divine appointment. What a monstrosity would develop if only one organ would do its part. vv. 18-19.

IV. *The interdependence of the body members. vv. 20-30.*
1. There is no such thing as irresponsible independence in either the physical or spiritual sphere. vv. 20-21.
2. Even the comely organs have their part to perform. vv. 22-23.
3. The several organs are God's workmanship looking to a unified action of the body. vv. 24-25.
4. All members share in the sorrow as in the joy of the body. v. 26.
5. The Christian Church is the body of Christ. v. 27.
6. Each of the various offices in the Church is to contribute its part toward the good of the commonwealth of grace. vv. 28-30.

Conclusion:—

For the good of the Church desire and exercise these spiritual gifts. v. 31 a.

>Lest the gift puff you up, give heed to the most excellent way. v. 31 b.

>>Like a mighty army
>>Moves the Church of God;
>>Brothers, we are treading
>>Where the saints have trod;
>>We are not divided,
>>All one body we,
>>One in hope and doctrine,
>>One in charity.

XVI.

THE GREATEST DYNAMIC — LOVE

I Cor. 13:1-13.

Introduction:—

"The most excellent way" opens up before us. Again and again the Apostle has sounded the warning that knowledge in itself is not enough. Spiritual endowments though ever so varied and useful are not sufficient. What is needed is "the expulsive power of a great affection." The secret of Christianity is its propelling force. Love is the great dynamic that furnishes power, purity, progressiveness. Of all spiritual endowments the most valuable is—love.

"The greatest, strongest, deepest thing Paul ever wrote is the hymn commencing with the words: Though I speak with the tongue of men and angels, but have not love, I am become sounding brass or a clanging cymbol. The new language on the lips of Christians was the language of love. But it was more than a language, it was a thing of power and action." Harnack, The Mission and Expansion of Christianity, I. p. 149.

"Love at the center has definite relation to the whole circumference of conduct. Love as the impulse of life produces the activities of love. Love being the supreme reason, all the deductions are also of love. Who shall write anything to describe the love-life after the poem of love from the pen of Paul ... Within the compass of that marvelous description, lies the most perfect unfolding of the fulfilment of law by love." G. Campbell Morgan, The Ten Commandments, p. 125 f.

I. *The excellency of Christian love,* vv. 1-3.
  1. It is more valuable than to speak the languages of men and of angels. v. 1. To speak these without while moved by love such speaking will lead to edification and will be marked by a tone and pathos that will give quality to the word spoken.
  2. It is more valuable than the display of supernatural insight and spectacular faith. v. 2. Comp. Matth. 7:22, 23.
  3. It is more valuable than just philanthropy. v. 3. Against this desire of distinction the Saviour directed some of his severest reproofs. Comp. Matth. 6:1-4. "The lifting force of social life is not compulsion, but like that of the planetary world, attraction... Many a disheartening experiment in well-intentioned charity forces a community or an individual to a re-examination of their own hearts. ... Christian charity surveys its problem from above, with detachment, perspective, and horizon." Peabody, Jesus Christ and the Social Question, pp. 263-264.
  4. Loveless men who show conspicuous power in respect to the exercise of gifts in the spheres of supernatural manifestations, spiritual influences, material aid will after all signify nothing, be nothing, gain nothing. Comp. *E.G.T.*

II. *The nature of Christian love,* vv 4-7.
  1. In setting forth the nature of Christian love Paul draws his illustrations all from its effect upon our conduct toward others, rather than in its manifestation toward God, because the need calls for a

specific exercise of this love toward others.
2. This description furnishes the mirror by which Christians of all ages can see the real merit of the love-life they profess.
3. Note the characteristics of love and observe its happy influences on mind and heart:
    (1) love suffereth long:—is "patient towards injurious or provoking persons." *E.G.T*.
    (2) love is kind:—"plays the part of a chrestos, (benignus), one who renders gracious, well-disposed service to others." *E.G.T*.
    (3) love envieth not: — "love does not envy others the happiness which they enjoy." *Barnes*.
    (4) love vaunteth not itself:—does not show off.
    (5) love is not puffed up:—"is not inflated with pride, and vanity, and self-esteem." The Saviour, who had most love for the human race, was the farthest possible removed from pride and vanity." *Barnes*.
    (6) love doth not behave itself unseemly:—"love imparts a delicacy of feeling beyond the rules of politeness." *E.G.T*.—Love "prompts to all that is fit and becoming in life." *Barnes*.
    (7) love seeketh not its own:—a striking and important expression that sets forth most beautifully the nature and power of real Christian love, fiinding its inspiration in the life of the Lord Jesus, "who went about doing good." Acts 10.38.
    (8) love is not provoked:—"prone to violent anger or exasperation." Love governs the temper.

(9) love taketh not account of evil:—"it is not malicious, censorious, disposed to find fault. Love will prompt to charitable judging." *Barnes.*

(10) love rejoiceth not in unrighteousness:—"to rejoice at iniquity when seeing it in others, is a sign of deep debasement (Rom. 1:32)." *E.G.T.* It neither loves the wrong, nor the fact that it has been done. *Barnes.*

(11) love rejoiceth with the truth:—"She rejoices in the progress and vindication of the Gospel which is the truth of God." *E.G.T.* Love does not rejoice in the vices, but in the virtues of others. *Barnes.*

(12) love beareth all things:—The more usual and classical meaning is to hide or conceal the faults and imperfections of others; the usage of the New Testament seems to demand that the word be rendered to mean forbear, bear, endure. *Barnes.*

(13) love believeth all things:—"not as encouraging universal credulity but that in regard to the conduct of others, there is a disposition to put the best construction on it." *Barnes.*

(14) love hopeth all things:—"hopes that all will turn out well. Love will hold on to this hope until all possibility of such a result has vanished." *Barnes.*

(15) love endureth all things:—bears up under, sustains, and does not murmur. *Barnes.*

III. *The permanence of Christian love,* vv. 8-13.

1. Love outwears everything. v. 8. "The charisms of ch. 12 and 14 are bestowed *on the way* and

serve the way-faring church, they cease each of them at a determined point; but the Way of Love leads indefinitely beyond them." *E.G.T.*
2. Prophecy, tongues, knowledge—faculties inspired, ecstatic, intellectual—are only partial in scope, and therefore temporary. But love will live. Let us seek then that which is permanent and eternal. vv. 8-10.
3. As is the transition from childhood to manhood, so is the transition from our knowledge at present to that breaking in upon us in heaven. v. 11.
4. Now we see but dimly and imperfectly, but then plainly and openly. v. 12.
5. Faith an dhope have meaning, subsistence and future only as love takes the initiative and supplies the dynamic of action. Where love reigns the sun never sets.

Conclusion:—

Love is the fadeless glow of the heavenly realm seeking to set our lamps aright. The gift of God's love provides the ground and basis of the Christian fellowship in which the present manifestations of love point to a land that is fairer than day:

"Where faith is sweetly lost in sight,
And hope in full supreme delight,
And everlasting love."
Charles Wesley.

XVII

EDIFYING SPEECH

I Cor. 14:1-40.

Introduction:—

This chapter signifies once more a descent to the plane of the rest of the Epistle. It is a continuation of the subject commenced in ch. 12, and pursued through ch. 13. The thought of the Epistle has been soaring high. But the practical issues are not lost sight of. The Christian fellowship is wrecked unless love holds sway. The exercise of "spiritual gifts," not equally bestowed upon all believers, call for a controlling principle such as love alone can furnish.

Any evaluation of spiritual endowments must take into account the cognate Christian truths as expressed in these related chapters—viz. the office of the Holy Spirit as the Church (12-31), and the sovereignty of love in the Christian life (13). Comp. *E.G.T.*

I. *Prophetic instruction excels unedifying speaking with tongues*, vv. 1-6.

   1. With love as the guide one had rather instruct the church intelligently than to loose himself in incommunicable mysteries. vv. 1-2.

   2. Prophecy consists of Spirit directed exhortation calculated to awaken the feeling and conscience of the hearers.

3. "Tongues" referred to in this chapter cannot mean foreign languages as reported in the description of the events connected with Pentecost, Acts ch. 2. Reproducing the argument of Fred. W. Robertson we urge against the adoption of the theory of foreign languages the following reasons:
   (1) if tongues represented foreign languages Paul would hardly call them less useful than prophecy, because they would much rather effect a marvelous opening for the Gospel.
   (2) it is clearly intimated that the tongues spoken of were inarticulate and incoherent, ecstatic rather than practical.
   (3) "Tongues" found expression, if at all audible, in an eternal, impassioned soliloquy, while foreign languages led to open and public declarations.
   (4) Tongues are like the sound of unworded and inarticulate sounds of musical instruments, while foreign languages would serve as vehicles of clearly formulated speech.
4. Prophecy is to be preferred because "Tongues" benefit nobody. While there is sound, there is no sense. v. 2.
5. While "Tongues" evaporate in vague mutterings," prophetic speech serves: (a) the further upbuild- of the Christian life, (b) the stimulation of the Christian will, (c) the strengthening of the Christian spirit." *E.G.T.*
6. Prophecy has the wider range of influence in the Church. v. 4.
7. "Talents are not to be estimated by their brilliancy, but by their usefulness." *Barnes.* v. 5.

8. Paul is ready personally to adopt the practical course. Not that he means to quench the spirit, but to build the church will be his primary interest. v. 6.

II. *Christian speech must find expression as a clarion call rather than in meaningless mutterings. vv. 7-13.*

1. One requires clearness of note even in inanimate instruments. v. 7.
2. The tone of the trumpet must be clear if the man in the field is to take his direction from its sound. v. 8.
3. v. 9 draws the inference: "As inanimate instruments by due modulation, and by fixed meaning attached to their notes, become expressive, so it is in a higher degree with the human tongue; its vocables convey a meaning just in so far as they are ordered, articulate, and conformed to usage." Quoted in *E.G.T.*
4. Speech must have clear meaning or one might as well be a foreigner to it. vv. 10-11.
5. Application turns to exhortation: seek spiritual gifts, not to satisfy selfish aims, but tto edify the Church. vv. 12-13.

III. Christian speech welcomes the disciplinary function of the intellect. v.. 14-19.

1. The consideration here brought in opens a new point of view, "The fruit of the speaker is found in the profit of the hearer." *E.G.T.*
2. Religious feelings and activities must use the intellect to find expression. v. 14.
3. Both prayer and song must be made articulate if the church is to profit by them. v. 15.

4. Spiritual utterances and expressions must be clear and intelligible if the Church is to give its hearty response. v. 16. "The united "Amen" seals the thanksgiving pronounced by a single voice, making it the act of the Church." *E.G.T.*
5. No matter how beautifully conceived, a spiritual message must be intelligible if the other person is to be edified thereby. v. 17.
6. Paul himself prefers to use every-day speech, as being the more serviceable. vv. 18-19.

IV. *A mad-house or a church, which?* vv. 20-25.
1. Overcome childish glee in unintelligible performances. Only be weak when it comes to evil things. Let all behaviour reflect a certain maturity of mind. v. 20.
2. As it was punishment for Israel not to understand the Assyrian tongue of the invader, so it is punishment to the Church if speech is employed which is not intelligible. vv. 21-22.
3. Unintelligible speech will lead outsiders to look upon the Church as a mad-house. v. 23.
4. Prophetic exhortation on the other hand will lead to the conversion of sinners. vv. 24-25.

V. *Christian services are to be marked by orderly procedure,* vv. 26-40.
1. "The holy Spirit is the author of order, and not of confusion (v. 33) and true religion prompts to peace and regularity, and not to discord and tumult." *Barnes.*
2. The rich variety of gifts will be orderly employed if to edify the Church is the dominant motive. v. 26.
3. That which cannot be made clear hath better be withheld. vv. 27-28.

4. Arrange the several parts of the service carefully. vv. 29-30.
5. The voice of prophecy must be trained by the word of prophecy. vv. 31-32.
6. The Christian woman, while keeping within her God-appointed place, will nevertheless cultivate a lively interest in spiritual things. vv. 33-36.
7. No one can plead ignorance of the declarations of God relating to these matters. vv. 37-38.
8. A last encouraging appeal for order and decency. vv. 39-40.

Conclusion:—

In the attainment of spiritual gifts we are utterly dependent upon the Holy Spirit. The carelessness with which they are said to manifest themselves in some circles at the present time has nothing in common with the unity and order insisted upon by Paul as demonstrating their genuineness of origin and intent. Spiritual gifts of the right kind can not be had for display. They are bestowed to help to edify the Church.

XVIII.

THE RESURRECTION OF CHRIST IN THE EXPERIENCE OF HIS FIRST FOLLOWERS

I Cor. 15:1-11.

Introduction:—

It is reported of Edwin Markham that the fire of his poetic genius flashed forth when at the age of fourteen he was required by his teacher to memorize a poem the first line of which ran: "When all the tombs of earth are tenantless." What an astounding faith this sentiment expresses! I Cor. 15 gives foundation and meaning to this challenging hope and outlook.

Chap. 15 does not stand in isolated aloofness to the rest of the Epistle. If the Cross was folly to the Corinthians, the resurrection even more so. Greek thought would readily embrace the concept of immortality, but the announcement of a bodily resurrection required keen analysis and sound proof. There was resistance to this idea too, because of the prevalent laxity of moral sentiment. The men who boasted superior knowledge were averse to Christian earnestness as reflected in moral tendencies, and their pride and spiritual arrogance led them also to discourage interest in the fact and faith of bodily resurrection.

It is Barth's contention that all hinges upon this chapter. It forms the very peak and crown of this Epistle. The argument has followed a steady course until it reached these heights. That is, all that has been said before, was spoken in full view of the resurrection fact. Here is the end which is at once the beginning. The beginning of what? of life, the only life that can change conditions such as spiritual pride and moral lapses. The life of these within the Church is a fellowship of the Resurrection. "Because I live, ye shall live also." This is not something on the periphery, this is the very heart of the matter.

I. *The fact of the resurrection is the foundation of the Christian message and faith.* vv. 1-2.

  1. The particle "now" R. V. ("Moreover," A. V.) (Greek-de) throws the subject into proper relief. While related to the general trend of the Epistle it marks nevertheless a sudden turn of thought of great importance. v. 1.

  2. Four steps lead up to the effective appropriation of this basic message and determining truth: The good news of the resurrection:

    (1) is preached to stimulate hearing and memory.

    (2) is received by admitting it as true.

    (3) furnishes a dependable basis to stand on as a vital and fundamental doctrine.

    (4) is indispensible to salvation, both present and future. "By this they were in fact saved from the condemnation of sin, and were in possession of the hope of eternal life." *Barnes.*

  3. The subject is more important than either the preachers or the hearers. The emphasis is upon the "Gospel" of the resurrection rather than upon the preacher or his hearers. This message is the

source, the basis, and the assurance of salvation. The Greek phrases used to indicate this relatedness to the main subject throws these words into bold relief.

4. Nor can the church afford to forget or corrupt this message. What is preached is to be kept in memory. v. 2. The Church is admonished to "hold fast" this word. Everything hinges upon the fact of the resurrection. The Church is undermining her own position and power when she loses sight of or corrupts this message. Christianity is empty and hollow when this truth has been surrendered. It is a good sign that Easter is made so prominent among us, but is that due to custom or the crisis brought on by and sensed in the fact of the resurrection? "If only the Word and the spark remain in our heart, it shall become such a fire as shall fill life, heaven, and earth, and consume both death and disaster like a drop of water, and so rend weak faith that no sin or death shall be seen or felt any more." *Luther*, quoted by *Barth*. p. 128.

II. *The fact of the resurrection is a pillar-truth of salvation.* vv. 3-4.

1. The four-fold method of appropriation is met by a four-fold delineation of fact. "The purport of what was delivered and received is described by the four sentences beginning with "that," to which four sentences all that follows, up to and including verse 7, is to be sensibly connected."

2. The "first of all" of this section is not to be read as being of numerical significance, but aims to

concentrate the attention upon the main, the central point.
3. There are sermons in tenses here. The verbal forms arouse our interest. "The death and burial are affirmed in the aorist, as historical events; the resurrection is put with emphasis into the perfect tense, as an abiding power." *E.G.T.*
4. "He died" is characterized by the "unhistorical addition" (*Barth*) "for our sins." That Paul could not have said if Christ's death were only an example of self-denial, because the reference to sin involves with yper-for, the notion of expiation. *E.G.T.*
5. The phrase "according to the Scriptures" is freighted with meaning. Therein is contained the whole history of redemption. From Genesis to Revelation these elementary facts stand in the foreground. "Christ died for our sins," and "rose again on the third day." These are pillar-truths of the Gospel. This was the message of hope as the fathers heard it. To this Jesus testified Himself in His conversation with the disciples on the Emmaus road. (Luke 24:25-32). All the light of sacred story gathers round these facts sublime. The Bible is consistent in its witness to a dying Saviour and a living Lord.
6. "He was buried." Christianity does not apologize for this "banal historical fact" (Barth). By His resting in the grave our Lord has hallowed the tomb. By going forth when it had been sealed He has given conclusive demonstration of the fact He has broken the bonds of death asunder. On the basis of this victory we are laid away to rest in hope.

7. "He rose" expresses according to Barth "the most serious objection to 'historical' interpretation." ... "On the third day," which definition indicates that "in His case restoration to life ensued, instead of the corruption of the corpse that sets in otherwise after this interval." Jesus appears to have seen a Scriptural necessity in the third day (Luke 24:46). *E.G.T.*
8. "The resurrection of Christ is another sign-board pointing to Christ crucified ... Resurrection must come to pass, or crucifixion will be of no avail." Herrick Johnson, The Ideal Ministry, p. 71. "The cross of Christ triumphs, in the hearts of believers, over the devil and the flesh, over sin and impious men, only when their eyes are directed to the power of the resurrection." Calvin, Institutes, Bk. III, chap. X, 6.

III. *The fact of the resurrection as testified to by eye-witnesses.* vv. 5-8.
1. "He appeared" (ophthe with dat. pass Aor., in reflecxive sense) is used of exceptional, supernatural appearances." *E.G.T.* This appearance is the direct object of the Christian testimony. With His appearance the new day has begun. Here is the new beginning. The verb indicates that the disciples recognized Him as they saw Him. As the fact of His death makes possible the forgiveness of sins ,so the resurrection announces to His disciples the certainty of His life and assures them of the possibility of continued fellowship with their living Lord.
2. "To Cephas" ... Paul cites the official witnesses. *E.G.T.* He refers only to the more important ones

and probably observes the exact order in which the Lord Jesus appeared to the disciples. *Barnes.* The reader of the Gospels will find it especially fitting that the risen Lord would manifest Himself to Peter at an early hour.

3. "Then to the twelve" ... still called so though Judas was now missing. To them He appeared in the absence of Thomas (John 20:19. 24); and when Thomas was present (John 20:24-29.

4. "To above five hundred brethren at once." "If the testimony of five hundred could not avail to prove His resurrection, no number of witnesses could." *Barnes.* Still living these could be appealed to as oral witnesses. Even the "falling asleep" of some encouraged in the hope of the resurrection, because it is expressive of the expectation of again rising.

4. "To James," the brother of our Lord, associated with Paul Acts 15:13, and 21:18. This manifestation explains the presence of the former unbelieving brothers in the circle of the 120 disciples. Comp. *E.G.T.*

5. "To all the Apostles." All participated in this latter sight, which coincides in point of time with Acts 1:6-12, not John 20:26. The witness of the First App. to the resurrection was complete and unqualified." *E.G.T.*

IV. *The fact of the resurrection as testified to by Paul himself.* vv. 8-10.

1. Paul also joins the ranks of the witnesses. He is not simply a continuer of this message, but to him also the living Christ has appeared.

2. "As to a child untimely born." Paul considered tirely abnormal. So little was he prepared for it

that he had no other explanation for it except to call it a miracle of the grace of God. But this he knew, with this experience life for him has its beginning.
3. Verse 9 explains how Paul is the abortion among the apostles; "in respect of his dwarfishness, and the unripeness of His birth into Apostleship." *E.G.T.* He considered himself unfit because he persecuted the Church—"a remorse which never left the Apostle." *E.G.T.*
4. Grace, utterly undeserved favour, has summoned Saul of Tarsus from the foremost rank of the persecutors to the foremost rank amongst the servants of the Lord Jesus." *E.G.T.* v. 10. Ready to admit his unworthiness, Paul never ceases to praise the grace of God which has counted him worthy. His success terminates not upon him, but upon the risen Lord Whom he has seen and to Whom he has been loyal. He has nothing to glory in except personal contact with the risen Christ. From that experience he will not swerve.
5. Grace was also the instrument that enabled Paul to excel in the work of the ministry.

Conclusion:—

"In the essential matters of vv. 1-4, and the crucial point of the resurrection of Jesus, there is not the least variation in the authoritative testimony. Peter, James, Paul—Jerusalem, Antioch, Corinth—are in perfect accord, preaching, believing, with one mind and one mouth, that the crucified Jesus rose from the dead." *E.G.T.*

XIX.

THE RESURRECTION OF CHRIST AS THE ESSENTIAL ELEMENT OF THE CHRISTIAN FAITH

I Cor. 15:12-34.

Introduction:—

This section, verses 12-34, demonstrates how important the fact of the resurrection is to Christian faith. The argument is precise, and sharply drawn. Every word counts. Faith is emptied of all cntent if the resurrection of Christ is doubted and denied. Without that assurance the Christian stands facing the abyss. Paul is bidding the Christian to consider what is to become of him if Christ were not risen. Atheism would be the natural result. To look past the risen Christ is to reveal that one has "no knowledge of God" (v. 34). Looking at the living Christ and the ensuing resurrection of believers however, it becomes clear that "God is all in all" (v. 28).

"One of the reasons why men believe the resurrection of Christ, will always be its supreme fitness to meet our human need of light upon the problem of life and death. By this it is that life and immortality have been brought to light. To those who cling to the conviction that human life must be worth something, that there must be somewhere permanent meaning and value in it, the resurrection of Jesus Christ is like the dawning of the day. It is congruous to the deepest and highest things in man, and as long as these things appeal to us, the credibility of the resurrection will draw from this congruity no small measure of support." Albertus Pieters, The Facts and Mysteries of the Christian Faith, p. 135.

I. *The denial of the resurrection empties faith of all meaning*, vv. 12-19.
   1. The hypothetical syllogism takes into account two parts: a) the falsity of the faith founded upon the resurrection, W. 13-16, and b) the unreality of the effects derived therefrom, vv. 17-19. *E.G.T.*
   2. The proposition stated in the form of a negative concession. v. 12. But the question is loaded with positive truth. The denial of the fact stands in flaring contrast to the general affirmation, as the very first word "now" (Greek-de) intimates. The preaching of Christ is felt to be inseparable from the preaching of His resurrection. To deny this is to stand in crying contradiction to the fact. "Christ is preached." The reading of the R.V. is to be preferred. The substance of the Gospel is that Christ rose from the dead. That which has appeared from God (the resurrection of Christ) applies to the whole of history within the scope of this horizon and addresses itself to us as God's revelation. Christianity without resurrection is a lie and deceit. Those that deny the resurrection saw off the branch upon which they are sitting. Comp. *Barth*.
   3. "If bodily resurrection is *per se* impossible, then there is no risen Christ." v. 13. *E.G.T.* "The absolute philosophical denial of bodily resurrection precludes the raising up of Jesus Christ." *E.G.T.* If we have to do only with natural events than

there can be no room for any resurrection, not even that of Christ. The fact of the resurrection is a link — perhaps the most important link — in the process of special revelation. Unless we are prepared to deny all revelation, we can not deny this special act. If we believe in God, we must believe in Christ also, in the risen Christ first and last.

4. If the fact is untrue, the testimony is untrue. v. 14. Then the witness of Christian preaching is void, unsubstantial, hollow. *E.G.T.* "There is something very touching in the manner in which the Apostle writes this monstrous supposition." *F. W. Robertson.* If Christ is not risen, preaching loses its content, "for *kerygma* is based on revelation, and revelation is in fact denied."

5. Then faith is also vain. v. 14 . "If the message is also empty." *E.G.T.* As far as Christianity is concerned all hinges upon this fact. If this conviction be sacrificed, the Church is but an empty shell and believers face despair. Christ can only be the object of worship and faith as He is the living Christ. If His resurrection must be denied then the Christian message has lost its content and dynamic power.

6. False witnessing in this matter dishonours God. v. 15. To affirm of God that He hath done what He had not done, namely to raise up an impostor would certainly discredit the character of God. Paul was very much conscious of his responsibility as a witness. If in ordinary matters false witnesses is a base and despicable thing, how much

more so when it concerns the truth of an eternal hope.
7. Verse 16 restates the position in order to press it to another, even more intolerable conclusion. *E.G.T.*
8. Two terrible consequences of a denial of the resurrection emerge:
   (1) ye are yet in your sins. v. 17. Christ's resurrection is the seal of our justification, and the spring of our sanctification (Rom. 6:4-11); both are wanting, if He is still in the grave. *E.G.T.* The picture is none too dark. We are face to face with reality. No human power can break the fetters of sin. Christ died for our sins and rose for our justification. There alone lies the deliverance from the power and guilt of sin. There can be no assurance and joy in the forgiveness of sin except there break in upon us the renewing power of a new world such as the resurrection of Christ promises and provides. Man is not cured of his sin by myths and the tricks of imagination. But the great objective fact of the redemptive power of the living Christ is adequate — and that alone. Escape from sin is only possible in fellowship with the risen Christ.
   (2) "they also that have fallen asleep in Christ have perished," v. 18. The sense of Christ's presence and the promises of His gospel turned death into sleep. Think of the emptiness of a faith that permits itself to be lulled to sleep when falling into utter ruin. Unless resurrection reaches into our life dy-

ing is a pitiful thing. We are facing nothing but corruption. But because of the resurrection of Christ we lay our loved ones away in the assured hope of the life with Christ forever.

9. Faith thus bereft of content and meaning has nothing but infinite bitterness in store for us. "We are of all men most pitiable," v. 19. Some are not ready to follow Paul in this assertion. It is said, that even if the hope of a resurrection should never be realized, Christians have lived happier and upon a higher plane than those disbelieving in Jesus. But that is speaking beside the point. The Christian life as such here and now lacks all foundation and meaning unless centering in the resurrection of Christ. Christian existence has no outlook or future if Christ be not risen. Our Christian confession is rather a mockery if belief in the resurrection should prove untenable.

II. *The certainty of the resurrection endows faith with joy and assurance,* vv. 20-28.

1. Having overthrown the contrary assertion, Paul now confidently affirms his unqualified faith in the risen Christ. Having weighed all the possibilities of doubt, he now returns to the joyful declaration of the fact. There is a resoluteness in his outcry which is as engaging as convincing, "but now hath Christ been raised from the dead." Quod erat demonstrandum.

2. The risen Christ is the firstfruits of them that are asleep. v. 20 b. The allusion is to the first harvestsheaf (Lev. 23:10). (Comp. Mt. 13:39 ff. John

5:28 f. and Rev. 14:14 ff.) "The first ripe sheaf is an earnest and sample of the harvest, consecrated to God and laid up with Him (cf. Rom. 6:10 f) in anticipation of the rest. The Resurrection has begun." *E.G.T.*

3. The contrast of Adam and Christ while making the identification of those fallen asleep a reality turns the attention in the direction of the great victory of the resurrection. vv. 21-22. The solidarity between Christ and the holy dead rests upon a firm and broad basis. Behold Adam with whom death, Christ with whom life begins. The present is pointing to the future. We are all concerned in the outcome. Doom stares us in the face if we have no share in the resurrection. The assurance of the fact is the promise of life to us. "Two doctrines are given to us in this text—original sin and original righteousness." *F. W. Robertson.*

4. Christ *and* the Christians are the participants in the resurrection of life. v. 23. "Tagna-order, signifies a military division; the Captain in His solitary glory (Heb. 2:10); and the rest of the army now sleeping to rise at His trumpet's sound (I Thess. 4:16)." *E.G.T.* Our present relationship to Christ is but an episode that leads to full realization.

5. The end of the reign of sin and death is in sight. v. 24. "When the clouds roll away we see both, sun and light, at the same time in one being." Luther quoted by *Barth.*

6. The resurrection of Christ points to the culmination of His kingship. v. 25. That Christ shall reign is to Paul a Scriptural necessity. His sove-

reignty will reach into every realm, including death. Death is Christ's opponent because He has come to bring life, and the fact that He is alive forever more, guarantees victory over the last enemy.

7. The resurrection deals the death-blow to death. v. 26. Death holds universal sway. But there is One Who is mightier. The risen Christ has destroyed the power of death and brought life and immortality to light. To those that say, there is no resurrection, the apostle replies: there is no death. The philosophy of denial is completely routed. "The dogma of unbelief has been confuted in *fact* by Christ's bodily resurrection (13 ff); in *experience* by the saving effect thereof in Christians (7); and now fiinally in *principle,* by its contrariety to the purpose and scope of redemption (21-26) which finds its goal in the death of Death." *E.G.T.*

8. vv. 27-28 are a supplement to vv. 20-26. Christ's dominion is unlimited. "Christ here stands forth the countertype of Adam, who forfeited our estate, winning for Himself and His own the deliverance from death (Heb. 2:9, 14 f.) which seals His conquest." *E.G.T.* Verse 27 reminds of the counterpart "It is finished," John 19:30.

III. *The announcement of the resurrection finds corroborating proof in the experience of believers.* vv. 29-34.

1. The practice of baptizing for the dead. v. 29. The verse is a *crux interpretum.* Several views have been suggested:

a) vicarious baptism. Believers were baptized for

those already dead. But we may be sure that Paul would never endorse this superstitious custom.
b) Calvin: those were also baptized who did not expect to live long, but had death in front of them.
c) those baptized would never have this rite performed upon them if baptism would simply mean the introduction into the community of the dead, which of necessity the Christian church would be, if it had no resurrection to proclaim.
d) Comment in E.G.T.: "Paul is referring rather to a much commoner, indeed a normal experience, that the death of Christians leads to the conversion of survivors, who in the first instance for the sake of the dead" (their beloved dead), and in the hope of reunion turn to Christ—e. g. when a dying mother wins her son by the appeal, "Meet me in heaven!"

2. The readiness to endure martyrdom proves the reality of faith in the resurrection. vv. 30-32. The oppressions of life are endured in the hope of the resurrection. "Fought with beasts" is not to be taken literally, because it is not mentioned either in 2 Cor. 11, or in the Acts of the Apostles. Barth sees in this the severe and exciting struggle with human powers. Comp. E.G.T. Only the understanding of the resurrection sees meaning in such fighting and suffering.
3. Loss of faith in the resurrection leads to despair and to moral recklessness. v. 32 b.
4. A denial of the resurrection exerts a demoralizing influence. v. 33.

5. Awake to the knowledge of God. v. 34.
Conclusion:—
> The strife is o'er, the battle done;
> The victory of life is won;
> The song of triumph has begun.
>   Alleluia.

XX.

THE RESURRECTION AS A TRIUMPHAL ARCH

I Cor. 15:35-58.

Introduction:—

"I believe in the resurrection of the body." *Apostles Creed*. "Should you go into the great cathedral of Milan, Italy, you would discover three great arched doors. Over one there is a wreath of roses under which are chiseled these words in Italian, "All that which pleases is but for a moment." You turn to the one on the left, and over it is the cross, and under that the words, "All that which pains is but for a moment." Then you stand before the great central arch and read this inscription, "That only is important which is eternal." J. C. Massee, The Ten Greatest Christian Doctrines, p. 105. Our chapter may be likened to this great arch. "Christ risen from the dead opens the kingdom of heaven to all believers." Watkinson, The Education of the Heart, p. 83.—Passing through this triumphal arch we make bold to say with Edwin Markham:

"I am done with the years that were: I am quits:
I am done with the dead and the old.
There are mines worked out: I delved in their pits:
I have saved their grain of gold.
Now I turn to the future for wine and bread:
I have bidden the past adieu.
I laugh and lift hands for the years ahead:
Come on: I am ready for you!"

I. *The reality of the resurrection pointed out by analogy,* vv. 35-42 a.
   1. The announcement of the resurrection is met by two distinct questions: Is such a thing possible? and: Does not the inconceivability of the manner of the resurrection strengthen the argument of the impossibility of the fact? v. 35. "The sceptics advance their second question to justify the first." *E.G.T.*
   2. Denial of the resurrection form betrays a sluggish mentality. v. 36. It is a matter of common observation that the seed sown, though decaying, issues forth into new life. Thus Jesus speaks of the grain of wheat which falls into the ground to die in order to bring forth much fruit. John 12, 24.
   3. If each seed develops into an appropriate grain, God will find a body for the one deposited to *decay.* v. 37-38.
   4. However great the variety of organic forms each has its own fit body. vv. 39-41.
   5. The various types of animals manifest this. v. 39. "If God can find a body for beast and fish, in the lowest range, no less than for man, why not, in the higher range, for man immortal no less than for man mortal." *E.G.T.*
   6. Heavenly beings have bodies fit to their condition. v. 40. Why not also the resurrection bodies?
   7. The several luminary bodies, reflecting each a particular glory, point to distinctiveness in the resurrection body. v. 41.
   8. V. 42 sums up the argument advanced. The resurrection of the dead "is as *possible* as that plants of wholly different form should shoot from the seed sown by your own hand; and the *form* of

each risen body will be determined by God, who finds a suitable organism for every type of life, in a region where, as sun, moon, and stars nightly show, the universal splendour is graduated and varied infinitely." *E.G.T.*

II. *The reality of the resurrection shown by the actuality of the resurrection body,* vv. 42 b.-49.
   1. Reasoning from analogy the Apostle had demonstrated that it was possible that the dead should rise. He will now point out several characteristics of the resurrection body.
   2. "Sown," "raised" . . . —"the verbs thrice repeated with emphasis, are contrasted in idea; the antithesis lies between two opposite stages of being." *E.G.T.*
   3. "Raised in incorruption" . . . The resurrection body shall be no more liable to decay, sickness, disorganization, putrefaction. *Barnes.*
   4. Sown in dishonour, it is raised in glory. The offensiveness of the grave will be turned into splendour, dignity, and honour. v. 43 a.
   5. Sown in weakness, raised in power. It will be no longer liable to disease, no more subject to infirmities and weaknesses which it here experiences, v. 43 b. "The corruptibility, dishonour, and weakness of man is, in fact, that of his corporeality. Death is the death of his body." Paul knows nothing of "some transition of man to a merely non-bodily existence."
   6. As the natural body performs its function in harmony with the present environment, so will the spiritual, the resurrection body in relation to the sphere in which it moves. v. 44. "A frame suited to man's earthly life argues a frame suited to his

heavenly life, according to the principle of verse 38 b." *E.G.T.*
7. This resurrection is not according to *our* logic, but according to God's order: "it is written." The resurrection is of divine origin. Coming forth from God, it terminates upon God and the results are in harmony with His being. God is a spirit. So is the new body sharing in the resurrection reality spiritual.
8. That creative power manifests itself in shaping the bodies of the two successive heads of the race. v. 45. By virtue of the first creation we stand in relationship to Him, who rose from the grave and who vouchsafes to us in his own glorious body our own higher and spiritual bodily existence.
9. The proper order will be maintained. v. 46. This verse "might have been expressily aimed at the Philonian exegesis; it affirms a development from lower to higher, from the dispensation of psyche to that of pneuma, the precise opposite of that extracted from Gen. I-II., by Philo." *E.G.T.* "That this must *happen*, is now stressed by the following verses, in which Paul, obviously in opposition to the speculations of Philo, but in opposition generally to a misconception which is very obvious here, emphasizes that the *spiritual* body is *not* the first."
10. Verses 47-49 draw another contrast between the two types of the two eras of humanity. "What Paul actually sets forth is the historical relation of the two Adams in the development of mankind, Christ succeeding and displacing our first father." *E.G.T.*
11. The relationship of hope exists, "we shall also bear the image of the heavenly." v. 48. The read-

ing "let us bear" (as in Rom. 5:1 "let us have peace") is false. It is not in our power to attain unto this image of the heavenly, but its restoration is of God. This looks unto the completion of the redemption wrought by the resurrection of Christ. This is the turning point from old to new. In the living Christ the lost image is restored. We are looking beyond the intervening years to the end when we shall see Him face to face and be like Him. The life and light of the new world are already upon us, and we are moving on into its full realization.

III. *The reality of the resurrection anticipated in the complete victory over death.* vv. 50-58.
   1. Verse 50 introduces with a pause, an emphatic reassertion of the ruling thought of the previous section. It is indispensible that we should have bodies different from what we now have. These two sentences cannot be utilized as proofs against the idea of bodily resurrection. The emphasis of v. 53 on the "this," which occurs four times, speaks distinctly against such a construction.
   2. The bodily resurrection is the result of a momentous revelation: "Lo, I show you a mystery." The evidence has been presented, rational proofs argued, now revelation reaches into the consideration of the subject to lift it into the realm of anticipated glory.
   3. The change will be universal. v. 51 b.
   4. The critical moment is defined by three vivid phrases:
      a) in a moment: "a point of time which cannot be cut or divided" (*Barnes*). It will be done instantaneously.

b) in the twinkling of an eye: also denoting the least conceivable duration of time.
c) at the last trump, suggests the solemn finality of the transformation. Comp. Matt. 24:31 f., I Thess. 4:16.
4. This sudden transformation is at once an *investure* with incorruption and immortality. v. 53. This verse urges the necessity of the change.
5. This clothing of the saints which the resurrection brings about, fulfils a notable O. T. word respecting the Day of the Lord: "He hath swallowed up death for ever," Isaiah 25: 8. "This is the farthest reaching of all O. T. prophecies; it bears allusion to Gen. 3. 3." *Dillman.*
6. The song of triumph, vv. 55-57:
   a) echoes the strain of Hosea 13:14.
   b) verse 56 throws into an epigram the doctrine of Romans IV.-VIII., and Gal. 3 respecting the inner relations of Sin and Law and Death. While Death gets from Sin its sting, Sin in turn receives from the Law its *power.* The Apostle was bound to link his theology of the Resurrection to the doctrine of salvation by the Cross. See *E.G.T.*
7. God giveth us this victory. v. 57. Thus we enter presently into the possession of the benefits of Christ's resurrection. We share in His triumph and sing the victor's song. We ought to be much more conscious of our eternal hope. Its apprehension should evoke joyful thanksgiving. Our deposit is sure. The glory of the new day lightens our path. While continuing to face the stern realities of life, our loads are lifted. Transcendant glory changes our outlook. Life has new mean-

ing, a new direction, and is overarched with a new radiance that beams forth from the sovereign majesty of the risen Christ.

Conclusion:—

"If the hope of the resurrection be removed, the whole edifice of piety would collapse, just as if the foundation were withdrawn from it." *Calvin.* Verse 58 briefly directs the previous teaching against the unsettlement caused by Corinthian doubts. *E.G.T.* This then is the crowning fact of fellowship with the risen Christ. We see deliverance from the domination of sin and death. We have imparted to us the hope of eternal life. We share in the triumph of Christ, and are encouraged to take up arms against the evil one. The fellowship of His resurrection establishes our heart and renews our zeal in the work of the Lord. We are urged on by a new motive power. We bring every problem in relation to the transforming power of His resurrection.

XXI.

THE RESURRECTION FAITH IN DAILY LIFE

I Cor. 16:1-24.

Introduction:—

The resurrection is proclaimed as a definite and overmastering fact. It provides a pivotal point in history. But it does not stand by itself in cold isolation. It asserts itself through supreme and creative consequences. It came to the disciples in a moment that bore them up by a new and overwhelming impulse.

The assurance of the resurrection gives direction to the practice of Christian faith in daily life. "Here is that power which, like the power-room in the engineering sheds, is carried to every part, and can work all the machinery, can accomplish the greatest and heaviest, and also the least and most delicate task that is required. The treatment of details is only an illustration of the way in which that central Power and Authority will always settle details." Horton, The Growth of the New Testament, p. 67.

The contents of this concluding chapter of the Epistle are of significance for the present time. "The whole account is as living, and fresh, and pregnant with instruction to us to-day as it was to the Corinthians of that age." *F. W. Robertson.*

I. *The offering as an expression of the Christian life,* vv. 1-4.
   1. The subject is implied in the text, "indicating this,

seemingly, as another topic of the Church letter (as in 7:1; 8:1; 12:1.)." *E.G.T.*
2. The history of this offering receives fuller treatment in 2 Cor. 8-9.
3. The word (offering) itself is variously expressed: as a logeia-club-contribution here; as a grace, v. 3; as a eulogia-praise, blessing 2 Cor. 9:5 (margin); as a leiturgia-service, 2 Cor. 9:12; as a koinonian-communication, Rom. 15:26.
4. "The fact that the collection is made for the 'saints' commends it to the saints." *E.G.T.* v. 1.
5. The method of giving is clearly indicated:
    a) it is to be systematic giving: "upon the first day of the week," "the earliest mention of the Christian day, going to show that the First Day, not the Sabbath, was already the Sacred Day of the Church (cf Acts 20:7), appropriate therefore for deeds of charity." *E.G.T.*
    b) it is to be liberal giving: "as God hath prospered him." Men do not give as God hath prospered them, because they do not give systematically." *F. W. Robertson.*
    c) it is to be universal giving: "let each one of you."
    d) it is to be thoughtful giving and not dependent upon chance or sudden impulse.
    e) it is to be prompt giving, to set minds and hands free for higher matters.
    f) it is to be directed through accredited channels, vv. 3-4. "This is the rule which Paul lays down here to guide the Christians at Corinth in giving alms—a rule that is applicable now, and as valuable now, as it was then." *Barnes' Notes.*

II. *The possibilities of pastoral work,* vv. 5-12.
  1. Pastoral work calls for ceaseless activity. vv. 5-6.
  2. Pastoral work calls for concentrated effort. vv. 7-8.
  3. Pastoral work acts upon the opportunity of the open door. v. 9 a.
  4. Pastoral work has to reckon with conflicts. v. 9 b. "Evangelism flourishes under fierce opposition." *E.G.T.*
  5. Pastoral work calls for an equal regard of all workers and helpers. vv. 10-12.

III. *The practice of brotherliness and ministering love,* vv. 13-20.
  1. The Christian life is characterized by the exercise of courageous qualities such as: watchfulness, steadfastness, manly vigour, Christian love. "The four imperatives of verse 13 are directed respectively against the heedlessness, fickleness, childishness, and moral enervation of the Corinthians; the fifth (14)—reiterates the appeal of chapters 8 and 13 touching the radical fault of this church." *E.G.T.*
  2. The family is the fundamental unit in the Christian enterprise. v. 15.
  3. Co-operative labours cement the brotherhood. v. 16. "Loyal and hard work in the cause of Christ earns willing respect and deference in the church." *T.G.T.*
  4. Christian fellowship brings the benediction of a refreshing and stimulating experience. vv. 17-18.
  5. Brotherly counsel will strengthen the work. v. 18.
  6. Christian greetings radiate good cheer vv. 19-20.

IV. *The Apostle's personal signature to authenticate the letter,* vv. 21-24.
 1. The title of the greeting, v. 21.
 2. The sign manual of the letter consists of four brief messages (Horton, The Growth of the New Testament, p. 68):—
    a) "Anathema" on the Lord's false lovers: recalls 12.3: "the haters of Jesus outside the Church inspired by Satan, call Him anathema, instead of Lord, and those who bow the knee to Him with a feigned heart are themselves anathema." *E.G.T.*
    b) "Maranatha," Aramaic for "the Lord is at hand," expresses the great watchword of the waiting Church. "The Lord Jesus will soon return to make investigation, and to judge the world. There will be no escape; and no tongue can express the awful horrors of an eternal curse pronounced by the lips of the Son of God." *Barnes' Notes.*
    c) the benediction, as (1) desiring them Christ's grace, expanded 2. Cor. 13:13 into the Trinitarian blessing; and (2) as assuring them his love: "My love be with you all in Christ Jesus." v. 24. "Many Corinthian Christians ranged themselves under other leaders, many criticized and opposed the Apostle, some he has been obliged to threaten with the rod (4:21); nevertheless he desires his love to all —and that abidingly, but in Christ Jesus, who is the basis and bond of love amongst his people." *E.G.T.*

Conclusion:—
"Herald of Christ, the day is come,
The page of life shall be unrolled."

"Receive every day as a resurrection from death, as a new enjoyment of life; meet every rising sun with such sentiments of God's goodness, as if you had seen it, and all things, new created on your account; and under the sense of so great a blessing, let your joyful heart praise and magnify the Lord."—*Law*.

"We have to be very practical in our consideration of Jesus. It never satisfied Him merely to introduce new ideals into the world. What He meant to do was to create new realities. His miracles of healing did not bring men beautiful promises and gracious comfort, but the great reality of most efficacious aid. And so in His resurrection victory over death is offered to those who 'through fear of death were all their lifetime subject to bondage' (Heb. 2:15). It is like a rock of granite on which the most fearful may feel secure." Otto Bochert, The Original Jesus, p. 452.